CW00937616

When Silence Speaks

£2

When Silence Speaks

The Spiritual Way of the Carthusian Order

Tim Peeters

DARTON·LONGMAN+TODD

First published in Great Britain by
Darton, Longman and Todd Ltd
1 Spencer Court
140 – 142 Wandsworth High Street
London SW18 4JJ

First published in 2007 as *Gods eenzame zwijgers: De spirituele weg
van de kartuizers*
by Carmelitana, 2007, Gent.

© 2007 and 2015 Tim Peeters

The right of Tim Peeters to be identified as the Author of this work
has been asserted under the Copyright, Designs and Patents Act 1988.

All photographs © Grande Chartreuse

ISBN 978-0-232-53202-9

A catalogue record for this book is available from the British Library

Phototypeset Kerrypress, Markyate, Hertfordshire
Printed and bound Bell & Bain, Glasgow.

Contents

Proofreader's notes

Many of the references in this book are from ancient sources. Every attempt has been made to preserve the integrity of the sources whilst ensuring that the text can be accessed in sound, readable English.

Scripture quotes in English are taken from the New Revised Standard Version Bible.

Abbreviations

AC   *Analecta Cartusiana*

Spir.Cart.   *Spiritualité Cartusienne*

SC   *Sources Chrétiennes*

Preface

This book will speak to you about a certain form of life which may appear strange or unreal because it is based on silence and solitude. These are two realities which many people try to avoid.

Nevertheless it may be that these states are necessary if one desires to deepen one's own life. Who can escape from this desire for any length of time?

In this sense, silence does not mean emptiness. Silence is a language that is nourished in solitude.

Silence does not mean absence and neither is silence a sounding board that echoes a word which would otherwise go unheard.

Silence prepares the way for happiness: a form of happiness which is born in one's own heart and soul. When the language of silence rises up, solitude becomes a necessity to fulfilment in life.

This book does not speak about strangers who live far away. Certainly they lead a life that evokes some puzzlement. This book speaks about each of us and the potential we have to enter into our inner self. This book invites you to find some time for silence and solitude in your busy life.

A Carthusian monk
+ The Great Charterhouse, June 2007

Introduction

O beata solitudo,
o sola beatitudo[1]

Arguably, no religious order in the Catholic Church
sparks the imagination as much as the Carthusian order.
The Carthusian monks lead a life of solitude, silence,
asceticism and prayer, hidden behind the high walls of their
monasteries and hermitages. What is the sense of such a
separate and pure spiritual life? What are they seeking in
the silence of the desert? Can we call the Carthusian way of
life a Christian and evangelical lifestyle? Is it not an escape
from the world, an escape from responsibility, a form of
complacency? These are some of the questions that arise
about monastic and contemplative life.

Those who visit the Grande Chartreuse (Grenoble,
France) or the tomb of St Bruno in Serra San Bruno
(Calabria, Italy) are certainly surprised about the great
number of tourists who try to catch a glimpse through
the doorways and dusty windows of this mysterious world

---

[1] Verse from the poem *Encomium solitudinis*, written in 1566 by the Dutch priest and
poet Cornelius Musius Delphius (1500–72).

beyond the locked doors and high walls. Some faces show their scepticism and disapprove of this strange, useless and seemingly anachronistic way of life. Others offer words of admiration, respect and even affection for these silent and solitary seekers of God. The German protestant theologian Rudolf Otto (1869–1937) called this fundamental human experience *'fascinosum et tremendum'*: fascination and fear, the dual perceptions of attraction and aversion that people recognise when they meet a reality that overwhelms their understanding.

June 1084 marks the foundation of the first Carthusian settlement in the high mountains of the Massif Chartreuse near Grenoble. On 6 October 1101 the *dies natalis* of St Bruno (born in Cologne, Germany, *c.* 1030), he founded the Carthusian order, in Calabria. These two historic dates were gratefully commemorated among the Carthusian monks with special festivities, colloquia, papal felicitations and even a pilgrimage by Pope John Paul II to the tomb of St Bruno. Today, more than 900 years later, across 22 monasteries, nearly 400 men and women, with authenticity and earnestness, attempt to live the ideal of St Bruno, who was a monk and hermit to the core of his being!

The mass interest in the film *Into Great Silence* (Philip Gröning, September 2006), which screened across the countries of the Western world, enlightened viewers to the reality of contemplative religious life. The film plunges the audience almost literally into the silent life of the Carthusian monks of the Grande Chartreuse. The popularity of the film suggests that the charism of St Bruno is still burning brightly. This unique documentary about the Carthusian life was called 'A movie like a monastery'. 'As a spectator, you undergo this silent life without much background information. The effect of such a silent movie is surprising. It is as if you are in the monastery itself.'[2]

Into Great Silence stimulates curiosity and the desire for a deeper understanding of this way of life, its history and its spirituality. Therefore this book will cover the spirituality of the Carthusian order as well as its history and actual lifestyle. Throughout the following three chapters we will introduce the spiritual foundations on which the Carthusian order is built. Spirituality comes from above, but is always lived from below. Spirituality is the mutual love story between God and humanity, in this case between God and the Carthusian monks. We will try to let them speak to you through the ancient spiritual sources and their own contemporary testimonies.

The design of the Carthusian order is above all the life work of two pioneers: St Bruno and Guigo I (1083–1136), the fifth prior of the Grande Chartreuse. Guigo is the author of *The Customs of Chartreuse*, on which the actual Carthusian statutes are based. We will set out with these two monks in the first two chapters. What inspired an important and highly intellectual person like Bruno, a professor and a canon in Reims (Champagne, France), to give up his promising and prosperous career in order to settle down as a hermit in the desolate and rough mountains of the Massif of Chartreuse? Bruno's two letters and his profession of faith reveal a certain glimpse of the deepest desires which moved him. Guigo I gave the primitive ideal of Bruno a juridical framework and he developed it for the next generations in

---

[2]   E. De Smet, 'Zwijgend bestaan', *Kerk en Leven*, 17 May 2006, p. 8.

his *Book of Customs*. In our time *The Customs of Chartreuse* are
the most important practical and organisational guidelines
for the entire Carthusian life.[3]

The last chapter is devoted to the proper spirituality
of the Carthusian order. Silence and solitude are the
fundamental principles. On a little plate near the gate of
the Grande Chartreuse is written, 'The monks, who devote
their life to God, thank you for respecting the solitude
and silence in which they pray and sacrifice for you.' The
Carthusian spirituality of solitude and silence began among
the ancient fathers in the desert. These hermits left the world
and entered the loneliness of the desert in order to find a
life with God. They were inspired by the experiences of
the desert found in Scriptures in the stories of the prophet
Elias, St John the Baptist and Jesus himself.

The spirituality of the desert received its own shape in
the Carthusian tradition. Three concentric circles are built
around the solitary and silent life of the individual monks:
the territory of the desert, the walls of the monastery and the
walls of the hermitage. Just as a medieval city was protected
by ramparts and moats, these three concentric circles protect
a sacred centre: the heart of each monk, which only God may
enter. The monotonous rhythm of life, the liturgy and *lectio
divina* (spiritual reading) are the pillars which keep the whole
spiritual structure upright. The daily benefit of such a desert
spirituality is not readily evident. This will become clear when

---

[3]   A Dutch translation of Guigo's *The Customs of Chartreuse* was published in 2011 by
Tim Peeters and Guerric Aerden OCSO. Tim Peeters wrote the introduction and the
annotations: cf. Guigo de Kartuizer, *Gewoonten. Een leefregel voor kluizenaars in gemeenschap*, (red. K. Pansters and G. Aerden) Budel, Damon, 2011.

we speak about the acedia, or listlessness, which appears as a struggle in each contemplative life on one day or another.

Visiting a Carthusian monastery or meeting a Carthusian monk is a rather exceptional experience. We want to thank them for their warm hospitality and open dialogue, which we experienced as special privileges. In the first place we thank Dom Marcellin Theeuwes, who was prior general of the Carthusian order from 1997 until 2012, and Dom Jacques Dupont, the former prior of Serra San Bruno. The conversations, the guided tours and the attendance at Mass or Vespers were a source of great inspiration. With gratitude we think about the meetings with the prior of Farneta (Tuscany, Italy) and the rectors of the Carthusian nuns of Nonenque (Languedoc, France) and Vedana (Dolomites, Italy). A very special word of gratitude to Dom François-Marie Velut, the former prior of Portes (diocese of Ars-Belley in France), who was elected prior general of the Carthusian order in 2012 (until 2014).[4] He gave us the opportunity to share the life of a real Carthusian community for more than two weeks during the summer of 2008. We keep in our hearts the memories we have of all the monks of the Charterhouse of Portes.

We want also to thank the anonymous monks of the Grande Chartreuse for writing the Preface and for the corrections to the original Dutch script of this book. We

---

[4] On 3 November 2014, Dom Dysmas de Lassus was elected as the new Prior General of the Carthusian order. Dom François-Marie Velut had to resign because of health problems.

also want to thank Sr Anne McGuire RSM (Australia) for her support with the English translation.

I

St Bruno and the Foundation of the Carthusian Order

Master Bruno

There is no authentic biography or hagiography in the strict sense available on the life of St Bruno. This means the lack of a life story which was written during his life or shortly after his death. All biographic facts delivered by the first generation of Carthusian monks on the life of their founder are historically correct, but very brief. Throughout the ages, history and legend became entangled. The sources do not reveal the precise date of Bruno's birth and they give no information about his childhood or youth. The only historical fact concerns his birthplace, namely the City of Cologne in Germany, somewhere between 1024 and 1031, most probably the year 1030. Therefore St Bruno is usually called 'Bruno from Cologne'. The first real biography on the life of St Bruno, written by one of the priors of the Grande Chartreuse, appeared as late as 1515 on the occasion of Bruno's canonisation. Due to the historical research of the Carthusian monk Maurice Laporte (d. 1990), we have an idea of the personality and character of St Bruno. The oldest biographic document, written by Guigo I, dates from 1130:

> Master Bruno of the German Nation, born into a well-known family in the city of Cologne, very learned in secular arts and theology, canon of the church of Reims, the primatial episcopal see of Gallia, and master of the Cathedral School, founded the hermitage of Chartreuse after renouncing the world. He presided over it for six years. Then Pope Urban II, one of his former pupils, requested him to join the Papal Curia, so that he might aid him with his counsel and support. As he was unable to sustain the chaotic conditions at the Papal Court, he left it to follow his yearning for the solitude that he had lost. He renounced the archbishopric of Reggio, to which the pope wished him to be selected, and withdrew to the hermitage of La Torre in Calabria. Although numerous lay and clerical persons crowded around him, he lived his ideal as a hermit until his death. About eleven years after he left France he died and was buried in La Torre.[5]

It is a historical fact that Bruno studied as a young noble cleric at the Cathedral School of Reims. As an extremely gifted student he obtained the degrees of magister and doctor in philosophy and theology. Later, he became principal of the Cathedral School and professor of exegesis. The reputation of his theological knowledge and of his eloquence as a

---

5   J. Hogg, Lives of Saint Bruno (AC 214/2003), p. 19.

teacher spread throughout Europe. 'Master Bruno' became an illustrious personality among European intellectuals. One of his former students is Pope Urban II (1088–99). The tradition attributes two biblical commentaries to St Bruno: one on the psalms and one on the letters of Paul. Most historians agree that none of these exegetical writings are from Bruno himself.

Throughout his academic career, Bruno was a canon in the chapter of Reims and also served as the bishop's secretary. These clerics lived in community and sang the liturgical offices in the cathedral. Around the year 1076, a dispute between certain canons and the new Archbishop of Reims, Manassès from Gournay, ran out of control. A part of the Chapter accused the Archbishop of the offence of simony[6] and they wrote a complaint to Pope Gregory VII (1073–85). In the spirit of the Gregorian Reform, which hoped for the end of all forms of simony in the Catholic Church, Manassès was suspended and dismissed in 1080. The canons beseeched the Pope to appoint Bruno as the new Archbishop of Reims. St Bruno refused this request.

Bruno as a hermit

Archbishop Manassès from Gournay was a very vindictive man, and he allowed the rifling of the houses of the canons and sold their goods and means of income. Therefore the canons had to flee from the city in 1076. Joined by two friends, Bruno lived a couple of years as an exile in

---

6   Trade in religious offices and functions.

the neighbourhoods of Reims. One of these friends was Ralph le Verd (the Green), who later became Archbishop of Reims. Far away from all occupations and duties, they had plenty of time to reflect and to converse with each other. On a certain day, somewhere in a garden, they took the common decision to leave the world in order to live a purely contemplative life as monks. But their resolution was never fulfilled. About twenty years later, Bruno wrote a letter to his friend Ralph to remind him of his promise:

1. Bruno, to the esteemed Lord Ralph, provost of the Chapter of Rheims: health in the spirit of true charity. I am aware of your loyalty to our long and constant friendship, the more wonderful and excellent as it is found so rarely among men. Great distances and many years have separated us, but they have not diminished your affection for your friend. By your warm letters and your many kindnesses to me, and to Brother Bernard for my sake, you have reassured me of your friendship, and in many other ways besides. For your goodness, I send thanks. Though they are less than you deserve, they come from a love that is pure.

2. A long time ago I sent a messenger with some letters to you. He was faithful on other errands, but this time he has not come back. So I thought about sending one of our monks to explain my concerns in person, because I cannot do it adequately by letter.

3. Now I want you to know – hoping it will not displease you – that I am in good health and things are going as well as I could wish. I pray God that it is the same for

my soul. In my prayer I await the divine mercy to heal my inner weakness and grant the blessings I desire.

4. I am living in a wilderness in Calabria, sufficiently distant from any centre of human population. I am with my religious brethren, some of whom are very learned. They persevere in their holy life, waiting for the return of the Master, ready to open the door for him as soon as he knocks. How can I speak adequately about this solitude, its agreeable location, its healthful and temperate climate? It is in a wide, pleasant plain between the mountains, with verdant meadows and pasturelands adorned with flowers. How can I describe the appearance of the gently rolling hills all around, and the secret of the shaded valleys where so many rivers flow, the brooks, and the springs? There are watered gardens and many fruit trees of various kinds.

5. But why am I giving so much time to these pleasantries? For a wise man there are other attractions, which are still more pleasant and useful, being divine. Nevertheless, scenes like these are often a relaxation and a diversion for fragile spirits wearied by a strict rule and attention to spiritual things. If the bow is stretched for too long, it becomes slack and unfit for its purpose.

6. Only those who have experienced the solitude and silence of the wilderness can know what benefit and divine joy they bring to those who love them. There strong men can be recollected as often as they wish, abide within themselves, carefully cultivate the seeds of virtue, and be nourished happily by the fruits of paradise. There, one can try to come to a clear vision of the divine Spouse who has been wounded by love,

to a pure vision that permits them to see God. There they can dedicate themselves to leisure that is occupied and activity that is tranquil. There, for their labour in the contest, God gives his athletes the reward they desire: a peace that the world does not know and joy in the Holy Spirit. Remember lovely Rachel. Although she gave Jacob fewer offspring than Leah, he preferred her to the more fruitful one, whose vision was dim. The offspring of contemplation are more rare than the offspring of action; so it was that their father had more affection for Joseph and Benjamin than for their other brothers. Remember that better part, which Mary chose and which would not be taken away from her.

7. Remember the lovely Sunamitess, that virgin who was the only one in the land of Israel found worthy to attend to David and warm him when he was old. I should like for you, too, dear brother, to love God above all, so that warmed by his embrace you may be aflame with divine love. May this charity take root in your heart so that the glory of the world, that captivating and deceptive temptation, will soon seem abhorrent to you; that you will reject the riches whose cares are a burden to the soul; and that you will find those pleasures, so harmful to body as well as spirit, distasteful.

8. You should always be aware of the one who wrote these words: 'If anyone loves the world and what is in the world – the concupiscence of the flesh, the covetousness of the eyes and pride – the love of the Father is not in him'; and these, too: 'Whoever wishes to be a friend of this world becomes an enemy of God.'

Is there any greater sin, any worse folly and downfall of the spirit, anything more hurtful or unfortunate, than to wish to be at war against the one whose power cannot be resisted and whose just vengeance cannot be evaded? Are we stronger than he? If, for the moment, his patient goodness moves us to repentance, will he not at last punish the offences of those who disregard him? What is more perverse, more contrary to reason, to justice, and to nature itself, than to prefer creature to Creator, to pursue perishable goods instead of eternal ones, those of earth rather than those of heaven?

9. My dear friend, what do you intend to do? What, if not to believe God's counsels, to believe Truth who cannot deceive? This is his counsel to you: 'Come to me, you who are heavily burdened, and I will refresh you.' Isn't it a burden both unprofitable and unproductive to be tormented by concupiscence, constantly under attack by the cares, anxieties, fears, and sorrows that are the result of those desires? What heavier burden is there than that which makes the soul descend from its sublime dignity down to the underworld, where all holiness is held in contempt? Then, my brother, flee all this agitation and misery, and go from the storm of this world to the cove where there is tranquil and certain rest.

10. You know what Wisdom herself says to us: 'If you do not renounce all your possessions, you cannot be my disciple.' Is there anyone who cannot see how beautiful and useful and pleasant it is to dwell in his school under the guidance of the Holy Spirit, there to learn divine philosophy, which alone can confer true happiness?

11. So, it is important for you to consider your duty carefully. If the invitation from love does not suffice for you, if the glimpse of useful goods does not impel you, at least let necessity and the fear of punishment restrain you.

12. You know the promise you made and to whom you made it. He is all-powerful and terrible, that Lord to whom you consecrated yourself in a pleasing oblation. It is not permitted to lie to him, nor is it profitable, because he does not permit himself to be mocked with impunity.

13. You will remember that day when we were together – you, Fulco le Borgne, and I – in the little garden beside Adam's house, where I was staying. We talked for some time, I think, about the false attractions and the perishable riches of this world and about the joys of eternal glory. With fervent love for God we then promised, we vowed, we decided soon to leave the shadows of the world to go in search of the good that is everlasting and receive the monastic habit. We would have carried out our plan had Fulco not gone to Rome, but we put it off until he would return. He delayed, and other matters came up, his courage waned, and his enthusiasm cooled.

14. What else is there for you to do, my dear friend, but to acquit yourself of this pledge as soon as possible? Otherwise you will have been guilty of a lie all this time, and you will incur the wrath of the all-powerful One as well as the terrible sufferings to come. What sovereign would permit one of his subjects to deny him with impunity a service that had been promised,

particularly a service he valued highly? Do not take my word for it, but believe the prophet and the Holy Spirit saying: 'Make vows to the Lord, your God, and fulfil them; let all round about him bring gifts to the terrible Lord who checks the pride of princes, who is terrible to the kings of the earth' (Ps. 76:12). Pay attention: this is the voice of the Lord, the voice of your God, the voice of the one who is terrible and who checks the pride of princes, the voice of the one who is terrible to other kings of the earth. Why does the Spirit of God teach that so strongly, if not to encourage you earnestly to do what you promised by your vow? Why is it hard for you to fulfil a vow that will not cause you to lose nor even diminish anything you have but will rather bring you great profit from the one to whom you owe it?

15. Do not allow yourself to be delayed by deceitful riches – they cannot relieve our poverty; nor by the dignity of the provost's office – it cannot be exercised without great peril to the soul. Permit me to say that it would be repugnant and unjust to appropriate for your own use the possessions of which you are merely the administrator, not the owner. If the desire for honor and glory inclines you to live in style – and you cannot afford those expenses on what you possess – do you not in one way or another deprive some people of what you give to others? That is not an act of beneficence or of generosity. No act is charitable if it is not just.

16. But I would like to discourage you from withdrawing from divine charity in favour of serving the Archbishop, who trusts your advice and depends upon it. It is

not easy to give sound, beneficial advice all the time. Divine love, being more sound, is more beneficial. What is more sound and more beneficial, more innate, more in accord with human nature than to love the good? And what is as good as God? Still more, is there anything good besides God? So, the holy soul who has any comprehension of this good, of his incomparable brilliance, splendour, and beauty, burns with the flame of heavenly love and cries out: 'I thirst for God, the living God. When will I come and see the face of God?' (Ps. 42:3).

17. My brother, do not disregard this admonition from your friend. Do not turn a deaf ear to the words of the Holy Spirit. Rather, my dearest friend, satisfy my desire and my long waiting, so that my worry, anxiety, and fear for you will torment me no longer. If you should leave this life – may God preserve you! – before having fulfilled what you owe by your vow, you would leave me destroyed by sadness and without hope for consolation.

18. That is why I beg you to grant my wish: at least come on a devotional pilgrimage to St Nicholas, and from there to me. You will see the one who loves you more than anyone else, and together we will talk about our affairs, our religious observance, and what concerns the good of us both. I trust in the Lord that you will not regret having undertaken the difficulty of such an arduous journey.

19. I have exceeded the bounds of an ordinary letter because, being unable to enjoy having you here, I wanted to talk with you a little longer by writing this. I

sincerely hope that you, my brother, will long remain in good health and remember my advice. Please send me The Life of St Remi, because it is impossible to find a copy where we are. Farewell.[7]

The letter of St Bruno needs to be understood within the historical context and theology of the Middle Ages. Certain images of God and a certain medieval piety seem quite strange today. However, this letter leads us to the centre of Bruno's desire and Carthusian spirituality: separation from the world and the contemplation of God in silence and solitude. 'Three elements of Bruno's desire for solitary life can be distinguished: the absolute primacy of God, the burning desire of his heart and the expectation of the coming of Christ. Bruno is guided by a deep understanding of God's Presence, adored and beloved above all other things. He is a man of singular desire. His inner peace shines on others. Many were touched by the simplicity and warmth of his personality. The image that Bruno gives of himself is characterised by a great inner stability and psychological maturity. Constantly he is nourished by waiting for the coming of the Lord.'[8]

The call to the Carthusian life is a call to leave everything in order to seek only God. In this abandon the monk encounters God. The basis of this call, as we read more than once in Bruno's letter, is the love from and for God. Bruno understood contemplative life as a time of hope

---

[7] St Bruno, *Letter to Ralph le Verd* (www.chartreux.org).
[8] M.Theeuwes, 'Bruno van Keulen. Ervaring en traditie', *Benedictijns tijdschrift* (2001/3), p. 107.

and expectation in anticipation of heavenly salvation: 'to expect and at the same time to possess, to desire and at the same time to rejoice, struggle and at the same time reward, desert and at the same time orchard, that is what Bruno understood as a pure contemplative call'.[9] Dom Marcellin Theeuwes, the former prior general of the Carthusian order, gives the following description of the Carthusian vocation: 'Our secret – if we have one – is to be found in the message of St Bruno, our founder. Throughout the ages he invites us to understand that the highest vocation of man exists in the contemplation of God ... By total surrender we receive the Absolute in loneliness and silence. The Carthusian monks pray for mercy for the entire world, for peace and surrender. We cultivate inner and external simplicity, in order to be more available to God and to receive everything from God.'[10] 'Our way of life is a search for the only thing which is really true in Christian faith, namely the love of God. For me, happiness is becoming totally transparent for God, without shadow or lie. Of course we aren't completely free of sin, we only try to live in the light of God without deceit ... Real happiness only is to be found in God. This profession of faith grants real peace. I, so small and poor – God, so mighty.'[11] In one of his homilies Dom Jacques Dupont, prior of the Carthusian monastery of Serra San Bruno, gives an interesting description of the proper meaning of contemplative life within the Carthusian tradition:

---

9   A. Ravier, *Saint Bruno le chartreux*, p. 173.
10   Article in the French Newspaper *La Croix*, 29–30 September 2001, pp. 4–7.
11   S. Pruvot, 'Entretien avec Dom Marcellin', *France Catholique* (2004/2915), p. 15.

St Bruno searched for God with his whole heart. That was for him the purpose of contemplative life. Bruno was a real contemplative soul and we as monks are also to be considered as contemplative men. In our age, the word 'contemplation' can have several meanings, but in Bruno's age contemplation always referred to monastic life. During the Middle Ages monastic life and contemplation became identical. In his letter to Ralph, Bruno uses the word 'contemplation' as a contradiction between the 'children of contemplation' and the 'children of action'. It is obvious that the children of action are all visible pastoral ministries in the Church – Ralph himself had one – and that the children of contemplation, although always fewer than the others, are the most beloved ones by God. Bruno's language is so clear that we cannot confuse it with significations out of other ages. He didn't understand contemplation as the Greek philosophers did, namely as an intellectual speculation of abstract ideas, nor in the way the mystic writers of the sixteenth century did, namely as an exceptional and elevated prayer … There is an essential difference between Christian contemplation and philosophical or theological speculation on God. A contemplative person does not stare to heaven but descends in his inner self. And in his inner self – the hell within us – he will find the mercy of God. He will find God present in the muddy abyss of his own being. God who became flesh and who is pure understanding, forgiveness and love. Bruno recognises that God is present in all human beings: God writes love and knowledge of his commandments in the hearts of men. Bruno recognises his own inner weakness and hopes that God's mercy will heal his soul.

To reach contemplation, a person must develop a clear eye. Nevertheless, one can have eyes and still be blind to see. The biblical Leah, who represents action, is short-sighted: she does not see as clearly as her sister Rachel because her eyes are obscured. If you want to see, you must open your eyes. Only then will you be able to bind the love of the Spouse with a serene look and you will see God as fully as God is. It is possible that Bruno was thinking about the pure-hearted men who could see God, but it is also possible that he thinks of these words of Jesus: 'When your eye is clear, your whole body will be enlightened. But when your eye is evil, your whole body will be dark.' A healthy and a clear eye will catch light and will enlighten the whole person. An unhealthy eye will only bring darkness.

We need new eyes in order to contemplate God. God gives sight through faith. But without love, our eyes are veiled and unable to see clearly, just as our faith is dead without love and good works. Contemplation is to see with the eyes of faith. No more and no less. Only the love in our heart can open these eyes so that we can see more clearly through the eyes of God ... The monk, who is filled with the love of God, will recognise God's presence. The eyes of his heart are enlightened. They are able to see God as God is. St Paul says that the connection between love and contemplation is natural: only when your love is big enough, will you know God. The more our heart is enlightened with love, the deeper will be our desire to see the face of God, our beloved one. Bruno, a man who burned with divine love, speaks of this desire through the psalm: 'I thirst for God who is life. When shall I rise, so that I will appear for God?' Bruno does not only wish to see the face of suffering, the face on the cross, the face of mercy and compassion. No, above all he wants to see the face of salvation and glory. This face of God reflects in my own face. In the exchange of these two different faces we will meet God perfectly.[12]

The modern reader of the letter of St Bruno will certainly be surprised at certain passages invoking an escape from a world of sin and depravity. These passages must be understood within the historical and theological context of Bruno's age. For Bruno, a radical break with the world and a definitive withdrawal to the desert was proof of total surrender to God. Solitude was a privileged place for an encounter with God. In Bruno's mind, solitude, silence, stability and self-denial were real virtues as well as conditions for reaching perfect happiness. For him, worldly things only provide fatigue and deception. So for Bruno the contemplative and solitary life was the highest stage of perfection.

In our time the Carthusians do not understand their separation from society as an escape from the world in a pejorative way, nor do they see it as a sense of misanthropy or complacency. Monks do not live in another age or in

---

[12] Un Certosino, *Ferventi di amore. Meditazione su San Bruno*, pp. 41–6.

space, in another dimension or on another planet. 'Our life is very simple,' says Dom Marcellin Theeuwes. 'As all men, we awake, we work, we eat and we sleep. The only difference is the concentration of all activities on God and prayer. The rhythm of our days seems quite monotonous, but it is not another dimension of time. The walls of our monasteries are not impenetrable: the news always finds a way in, often by people who work for us. We were immediately informed about the attacks of 9/11. We prayed all day ... Also during spring 2003, when the war in Iraq was a fact, we prayed a lot because we also felt the tension of humanity. Our community knows what happens in the world because we read articles in certain magazines, but we never watch images on television.'[13] On top of one of the letters we received from Dom Marcellin Theeuwes was written: '+ En Chartreuse, le 11 (sic!) Septembre 2006': 'Yes indeed! Today, 9/11!' 'Deprived from all, allied with all' is a famous aphorism in the statutes of the Carthusian order.

Cardinal Godfried Danneels, the emeritus Archbishop of Brussels, says that monks leave the world because they give priority to God, not to creation. 'Only God is absolute. For this reason, monks settle down in lonely places. Even as a community they establish moments of individual solitude. They fulfil the words of Abraham: "Leave your country, your house and family" (Gen. 12:1). Monks indeed leave their country, their home and family. They renounce all secular things in order to confess with inner strength that the riches

---

[13]   P. Drijvers, 'De weg naar het wezenlijke. Gesprek met de prior van La Grande Chartreuse, Marcellin Theeuwes', *Monastieke Informatie* (2004/211), p. 108.

of the Kingdom of God are much more important. Monks are poor, pure and obedient. Not because of its efficiency, but because of the Kingdom of Heaven. Each and every day of their lives, monks direct themselves towards heaven. They are like trees deepening their roots. They do not live in the past or in the present, but in the future. Their whole life is directed to just one goal: contemplation. Through faith they see already what we all shall see in heaven: the contemplation of God.'[14]

Carthusian monks leave the world in a very radical way. Cardinal Danneels offered profound reflection on the film *Into Great Silence*:

> Carthusian monks give up everything, even their own individuality and their personal freedom. For most people it seems impossible, but for those who believe they received all things, it is not so difficult to do. Nothing we possess belongs to us, because everything is given by God, the Creator of all things. For this reason, Carthusian monks have respect for the most banal material things. In the film we notice how each single button or piece of silk is being reused. Nothing is wasted because everything is a gift from God. Of course there are other reasonable ways of doing. But in faith, there are no limits. There is only a floor, but no ceiling. All people will confess their faith according to their own capacities. Each of us has to

---

[14]   G. Danneels, 'De laatste en de voorlaatste dingen', in Abdij van Westmalle, *Stilte aan het woord*, pp. 83–4.

be prepared to give up something if we want to follow Christ. Religious forsake family and certain personal freedoms. The Carthusian monk has a different calling: he forsakes public life, individual freedom and material possessions. Just like a Buddhist monk, he chooses total surrender. But once again, he can do this because he has the capacity to do so.[15]

But let us return to the Middle Ages, the age of St Bruno. Bruno left Reims probably around 1082–83 in search of an appropriate place for solitude. He set himself up as a hermit in the woods of the Benedictine abbey of Molesmes, at the border of Champagne and Burgundy, accompanied by two others. Robert, the Abbott of Molesmes who later was to found Cîteaux, gave them a rather desolate spot on a property which was called *Sèche-Fontaine* (Dry Fountain). However, the silence and solitude were constantly interrupted by visitors. Therefore Bruno left the abbey of Molesmes quite soon after in search of a better place, more desolate and sparse, in order to realise his dream. At the beginning of 1084 he marched in the direction of the French Alps.

Bruno the Carthusian

When Bruno arrived in the city of Grenoble, he immediately visited Bishop Hugo from Châteauneuf. It was the bishop who personally guided Bruno and his six companions into the mountains of the Chartreuse massif. This magnificent

---

[15]   M. De Roeck, *Kardinaal Danneels over Into Great Silence*, pp. 1–2.

chain of high mountains lies in the French department of Isère, more precisely in the Dauphiné, the south-west region between the Alps, the river Rhône and Provence. It was June 1084, Bruno was nearly 54 years old. This 'genesis story' was written by Guigo I in his *Biography of Saint Hugo*, the Bishop of Grenoble: 'They arrived, driven by hope and attracted by the sweet perfume of holiness of the bishop. The bishop received them with respect and joy, he discussed with them and he confirmed their desires. With the guidance of his counsel, help and company, they penetrated into the desert of Chartreuse and there they started to build.'[16]

The statutes of the Carthusian order, approved in 1991 by the Vatican, start with a reference to the year 1084 as the birth year of the Carthusian family: 'To the praise of the glory of God, Christ, the Father's Word, has through the Holy Spirit, from the beginning chosen certain men, whom he willed to lead into solitude and unite to himself in intimate love. In obedience to such a call, Master Bruno and six companions entered the desert of Chartreuse in the year of our Lord 1084 and settled there; under the guidance of the Holy Spirit, they and their successors, learning from experience, gradually evolved a special form of hermit life, which was handed on to succeeding generations, not by the written word, but by example.'[17] Even today, seven stars symbolise the seven pioneers of the Carthusian tradition in the escutcheon of the order, which represents a globe and an erected cross on top of it. The aphorism *'Stat crux dum*

---

[16]   Un Chartreux, *La Grande Chartreuse*, p. 247.
[17]   Statutes of the Carthusian Order, 1.1.

volvitur orbis', in translation 'In the rotation of the world, the Cross remains immovable', became the proper symbol of the Carthusian monks.

The natural position of the Chartreuse massif, the inhospitable heights and the rude climate opened in the eyes of Bruno the main gate of Paradise. A narrow gap between the high rocks was the only entrance to this wilderness of huge forests, dangerous ravines and deep waterfalls. The flanks of the mountains are covered with snow and fog for more than six months each year. Through reading the famous book *La Grande Chartreuse*, the anonymous author, a Carthusian monk, enables us to follow the journey of Bruno and his companions through the savage Chartreuse massif:

> Nowadays the usual road to reach the Chartreuse massif runs from the village of St Laurent du Pont. But this road did not exist in the Middle Ages. In the eleventh century – and until much later – the desert of Chartreuse was more desolate than it appears today. St Bruno and his six companions left Grenoble and began to climb beyond the village of Le Sappey. Passing by the last hamlets of the village, they passed beyond the edge of Palaquit to reach the highest point of their journey, the edge of Porte (4347 feet). From there they descended beyond the village of St Pierre de Chartreuse. The whole road ran through dense forests which today still exist for the most part. The actual road follows nearly exactly the primitive route. They passed St Pierre de Chartreuse on the left-hand side and they set foot upon the small gorges of the Guiers Morts, which are cut out between two steel and

sheer flanks and which give barely space for a river and a road. In the foundation act of the monastery this mountain pass is called *Rocky Gap*. According to the ancient Carthusian documents *Rocky Gap* was the only access to the desert. Nowadays it is possible to cross the gorges by a bridge which is called *the bridge of Rocky Gap*.[18]

Pilgrims and tourists who visit the Chartreuse massif and the monastery of the Grande Chartreuse will recognise the atmosphere immediately. The roughness of nature, the impressive valley between the rocky mountains, the thick snow banks during winter, the resounding thunders and the heavy rains, the screaming of birds of prey in the sky and especially the omnipresent silence, on which road signs are found with the clear message, 'Zone of Silence'. All this provides a constant reminder and a deep understanding of that solitude for which Bruno was searching. Those who dare to battle the heavy climb to the place of the original cells will have an even better understanding of why this desolate place was a paradise of silence and solitude in the mind of Bruno. On the site of the original cells, there are only trees, clouds, birds and God as company. When Bruno took the decision to settle down in the Chartreuse massif, he did so because the natural environment of this place reflects a strong similarity to his spiritual aspirations. For Bruno the Chartreuse massif evoked the essence of his desires. His heart was ready for a radical decision. This decision reveals

---

[18]   Un Chartreux, *La Grande Chartreuse*, p. 247.

the content of his soul at that particular moment: only God. Bruno left all compulsion behind in order to find a certain independence from those things which shackle and imprison humanity. He is a strong example of a person who is anchored within the depths of his soul. He shows us that there exists no foundation but God alone. Our roots do not lie in our own achievements, our actions, our relationships.'[19] 'Bruno knew well the passages in the Psalms and the Books of Wisdom which evoke the beauty of nature and its cosmic majesty. God rules all elements of creation. Bruno experienced this divine reality in the deepest centre of his soul. So I can imagine that Bruno shouted: "This is it!" or the Greek "Eureka – I have found it!" when he entered the Chartreuse massif.'[20]

Leo Fijen, a Dutch journalist who made a documentary about Dutch abbots and abbesses in different European abbeys and monasteries (2004), had the same experience when he met with Dom Marcellin Theeuwes for an interview in the Grande Chartreuse:

> Dom Marcellin walks with me to the spot where St Bruno began this austere life in 1084. The landscape is quiet and stark, desolate and erratic. We are in the high mountains, far above the monastery of the Grande Chartreuse. Several huge rocks lie down in the greenery. These rocks fell down as a result of an avalanche many centuries ago. Most of the first Carthusian monks

---

19   P. Drijvers, *De weg naar het wezenlijke,* pp. 102–4.
20   S. Pruvot, *Entretien avec dom Marcellin,* pp. 12–13.

were killed. Afterwards the three surviving monks went down into the valley to a safer place, to the site of the actual monastery. I am aware of the fact that we stand on sacred soil. Marcellin Theeuwes even lowers his voice: 'Bruno was in search of abandonment so that he could find the most essential thing in life. Here, in the middle of pure desertion, you can only listen to your own heart. Only in your own heart you will get to know yourself and you will find God. That was the only goal of Bruno's life and also of mine.'

Whoever enters the Chartreuse massif leaves the world behind. In this place one experiences real aloneness and silence. In the mountains of the French Alps around Grenoble there is nothing except rugged rocks and narrow, dark tunnels. At the left and right sides there are only mountains which make the road desolate and eerie. In passing the bridge of St Bruno one encounters a blind alley. Despite all this, thousands and thousands of people make this journey each year. They all move in the same direction, into the high mountains, into the rugged desert. They want to see with their own eyes the most severe isolated monastery in the world, just as I too want to see! But as a tourist or a pilgrim, the view does not come free! You have to walk through the forests, for nearly two miles, while silence and solitude receive you as their guests. To really understand the secret of this severe monastery, one has to slow down and adjust to the slower pace of the monks.[21]

Bruno and his companions built a primitive monastery at an altitude of 3,590 feet in close proximity to flowing water. Each hermit had his own wooden cottage which looked like the alpine cottages of the woodcutters. Strong roofs had to protect each hermitage against rain, snow and wind. They had thick wooden walls and small windows to keep out frost. Each cottage had an open fire. A covered gallery connected the different hermitages to the church, which was the only building made of stone, where the monks gathered for morning and evening prayer. They prayed, worked, ate, studied and lived for most of the day in total solitude and silence. The physiognomy of the Carthusian life and the typical architectural structure of a Carthusian monastery, whereby the different hermitages are connected with the other parts of the monastery by a cloister, were born here in their most primitive form. The birthplace of the Carthusian order is called *Casalibus*, which means 'from the cottages'. On the spot of the original church is built the chapel of Our Lady of Casalibus.

Among the companions of Bruno four were clerics and two were laymen. For this reason the difference between the priest monks and the lay brothers (friars), who are called *converses*, is as old as the Carthusian order.

Both try to find unity with God, but each in their own way. From the beginning of the order in the eleventh

---

[21]   L. Fijen, *De reis van je hoofd naar je hart. Leefregels voor het bestaan van alledag*, pp. 127–8.

century the friars protected the solitude of the monks. But also their own solitude was guaranteed, as they lived within the territory of the desert. For several centuries the friars lived strictly separated from the cloistered monks, but nowadays they live in the same monastery.

As time passed a third category of religious arose: the so-called *donnés* or the 'donate brothers'. Initially they were simple workers in the service of the community, but later on they became real monks: they wore monastic habits and lived a life similar to the converses. But they were not bound by vows. They 'gave' themselves to the monastery because they loved Christ and they made a promise to serve God. The original Carthusian community combined these three different lifestyles as both complementary yet inseparable parts. Monks and converses had a very distinct lifestyle. The monks lived in the secrecy of their hermitage, while the converses, within their vocation for solitude and prayer, took care of all material affairs and manual labour. Without the contribution of both specific roles the Carthusian order would not be the same. Therefore it is impossible to reduce Carthusian life to one of these parts because it exists in the unity of both lifestyles.[22]

At the time of Bruno the converses lived in a distinct building, which was called the 'lower house' or the 'inferior

---

[22]   Un Chartreux, *La Grande Chartreuse*, pp. 38–9.

house', because it was located about 1,000 feet lower in the valley. The friars had their own cells, their own chapel and several workplaces. They formed in a certain way a natural buffer for the quiet and order in the 'higher house'. Bishop Hugo conferred a property of 1,700 hectares to the Carthusian community – enlarged even later on – in order to afford it protection under the law. Within the border of this territory only the Carthusian monks – and no one else – had exclusive possession of all rights. Each intruder was punished with excommunication.

In the place where the converses lived in former times, there is a museum (founded in 1957 and totally renewed in 2011). The Museum of the Grande Chartreuse gives a realistic impression of Carthusian life within the cloister walls. Nearly 65,000 tourists and pilgrims visit the museum each year. The monks are still surprised that even after a visit many myths and fantasies remain. 'The myths about our lives still surprise us,' says Dom Marcellin Theeuwes. 'The sparse communication with the outside world and the attachment to solitude probably nourish these myths. But for we who live inside the cloister walls, life is quite prosaic. The media are usually interested in the extraordinary aspects of our life. They like to emphasise that we have a severe and tough life. But for us, the essence of our life is to be found elsewhere. Our daily rhythm is the result of a very wise balance.'[23] 'We have nothing to hide. This would be a false image. Some people even think that we are a kind of secret society. But our life is very transparent:

---

[23]   S. Pruvot, *Entretien avec dom Marcellin*, p. 13.

we have nothing to hide! We only try to remain discrete because we try to protect the benefits of separation. We all possess a secret garden in ourselves: our heart where we meet the intimacy of God. Even facing the other monks we remain discrete about our personal relationship with God. Sometimes we share personal familiarities with each other during our weekly walks. We even have the opportunity for a deeper exchange. When I visit a monk in his cell, especially the young, we communicate very openly about intimate affairs. But the personal relationship with God is private and we respect this secret. It belongs to the level of the inexpressible..[24]

The rough climate and the poor soil in the high mountains of the Chartreuse massif made the life of the first Carthusians very austere and unpredictable. A field in the rocky soil produced some vegetables, grains and fruits, but never enough to get through winter. A herd of cattle and a few chickens provided dairy products, wool and parchment for the copy of books, which was the main form of labour in the primitive Carthusian tradition. Fish were caught in the mountain rivers but the vegetarian content was quite sparse. A community that lived in these conditions could not be numerous of course. That's why Guigo I introduced a *numerus clausus* of 13 monks and 16 converses. Otherwise it would be impossible to maintain independence from the outside world. The rule of a *numerus clausus* is found also in other monastic orders, for example the Carmelite nuns. In order to protect the autonomy of a Carthusian community

---

[24]   P. Drijvers, *De weg naar het wezenlijke*, pp. 114–15.

as well as possible, Guigo I forbade the acceptance of gifts, presents, incomes and even the possession of fields or buildings outside the territory of the monastery. When a community was no longer able to provide for its own proper sustenance, the number of residents had to be reduced:

> The number of residents in our hermitage is precisely fixed at thirteen monks, though it is not our desire to maintain the same number of residents – for the moment we are even less – because we are open to receiving all candidates whom God sends to us. So when a candidate of great benefit and virtue wants to join us, we will accept him as a fourteenth resident so long as the supplies of the community allow us to do so. The number of lay brothers decided on is sixteen. For the moment we have more. But some of them are old or demented and unable to work. That is the reason for accepting new friars. But when the weaker ones die, we will not accept any new candidates.
>
> We have chosen this small number because the benefits of the natural sources on this place should never force us to beg or to wander to practices we despise. When those who will come after us for unknown reasons cannot manage with the sustenance of the religious community without the dangerous practice of begging and wandering, they must reduce the number of residents in order to be protected against these dangers ... We do not accept any gifts, because we do not want to gain uncertain profits by accepting risky commitments we may have to discharge or to accomplish. Agriculture and cattle breeding –

and no gifts – must enable us to survive with a small number of men in this desert. This rule is also in force with regard to humility, poverty, a moderate lifestyle, clothes and all other things we use. Day by day we have to increase our separation from the world and our love for God. Only for God we have to endure everything.

May God help us to avoid all kinds of greed. Therefore we forbid, with this writing, the possession of anything whatsoever outside the limits of the desert: no fields, no vineyards, no gardens, no churches, no cemeteries, no offers, no tithes, in one word nothing of this kind.[25]

Even today the Carthusians try to stay true to this stark rule in most monasteries. 'The small number was necessary for the development of the Carthusian life and order. Throughout the ages it was an excellent protection for our stability. It became a cornerstone of our vocation and spirit', testifies a Carthusian monk. 'The small number benefits our lifestyle. The Carthusians must keep this rule for ever. They must avoid the temptation to be numerous and never complain about being small in number. Bruno started with only six men in the desert of Chartreuse! This example must encourage us never to derail.'[26]

Two well-preserved written observations by eyewitnesses from the beginning of the twelfth century are an important historical source about the life of the first monks in the

---

25   *Customs of Chartreuse*, 78, 1–2; 79, 1–3; 41, 1.
26   Correrie de La Grande Chartreuse, *Paroles de chartreux*, p. 146.

high mountains of Chartreuse. One of these eyewitnesses was Petrus Venerabilis, the abbot of Cluny, who left us this impression: 'According to the ancient customs of the Egyptian desert monks they live in separate hermitages. They devote their lives to study, prayer and labour, especially the copying of manuscripts. Silence is never interrupted. When the bell rings in the church tower they pray the usual offices in their cells: Prime, Terce, Sext, None and Compline. They gather in church for Vespers and Matins.'[27]

The second eyewitness is Guibert from Nogent, a Benedictine abbot:

> The church is built on a rock. Around the church different hermitages are built, in which the monks work, sleep and eat separately. Each Sunday they receive provisions from the administrator, namely bread and vegetables, the only nutrient they eat boiled. Each monk cleans and prepares the vegetables for himself. They take water out of a streamlet, which flows along the hermitages and is directed into the cells by gutters. Only on Sundays and feast days do they receive fish and cheese. Fish only when it is received as a gift, because they do not buy anything. They do not go to church at the usual times like others do, but only during certain moments of prayer. They almost never speak. They use gestures when they need something. The soil is poor and unfruitful, so they have just a few cornfields. But they have a large herd of livestock

---

[27]   UN Chartreux, 'Introduction', in *Coutumes de Chartreuse*, p. 12.

which they sell to provide for their sustenance. They live totally separated from the world while they aim for perfection.[28]

Throughout the centuries the monastery of the Grande Chartreuse was eight times struck and destroyed by fire. Dom Innocent le Masson, who used to call himself 'le maçon' or ' mason', built the actual monastery in 1676. It was entirely built from natural stone and fire-proof slate tiles. It took more than 12 years to realise this massive complex of buildings. The Grande Chartreuse embraces no less than 35 hermitages and enough bedrooms to accommodate the priors of the nearly 170 monasteries during the seventeenth century as they gathered every two years for the general chapter. The history of the Grande Chartreuse is not only published for adults, but also for children as an attractive and readable comic.[29]

Bruno chose a white monastic habit, quite similar to the clothing of the poor farmers and mountaineers in the region. The typical Carthusian habit has two large parallel ribbons at the hips, connecting the front and back parts of the scapular. These ribbons symbolise the devotion to God towards monastic vows. That's why a novice's habit doesn't have these ribbons yet. Each habit has a big cap and a leather belt. The friars wear similar habits.

It is quite clear that Bruno made a very radical choice for solitude. He was able to do this because he had

---

[28]   W. Nigg, *Het geheim der monniken*, p. 180.

[29]   Cf. L. Bidot, *L'histoire de la Grande Chartreuse en BD*, 2001.

a maturity made rich by life experience. He gave the divine dimension the optimal space for growth in his life. Solitude enabled him to make sense of his life: to be totally available for the divine love. Certainly he made a choice for a high degree of solitude in human interactions, but at the same time he received in equal measure communion with God. What seems to be absent on the one hand is supplied with infinitely more depth on the other. Sometimes, people must reach their limit before they can taste the total depths of their own eternal being. Solitude as a life choice is a very strong symbol of this limit … Bruno did not only make the choice for separation from the world, but he also established a small community in which each individual monk could devote the largest part of the day to silence and solitude. This aspect of solitude is a determinant for Carthusian life. Not as an absolute solitude, but as a dominant one. Solitude is the most typical characteristic of Bruno's foundation. It is not surprising that the local population called Bruno *the hermit* and that the first Carthusians called their monastery *a hermitage*.[30]

'Solitude is the most inherent element of the Carthusian vocation and lifestyle. Solitude renders them a proper identity within the broad spectrum of religious lifestyles in Christianity throughout the ages.'[31]

---

[30] M. Theeuwes, *Bruno van Keulen*, pp. 106, 113.
[31] P. Nissen, *Eenzaamheid als zoeken naar God*, p. 90.

Bruno as papal counsellor

In the year 1090 Bruno was called to Rome by his former student Pope Urban II. He was asked to assist the Pope as a counsellor in the governance of the Catholic Church. Urban II, a foreign monk of the abbey of Cluny, was a fervent supporter of the Gregorian Reform. He wanted to put an end to investiture, simony and concubinage of priests and bishops. But his pontificate was constantly overshadowed by the conflict between the German emperor Henry IV and the antipope Clement III (1080–1100). Soon after his election Pope Urban II had to fight for the imperial army and withdraw to an island in the Tiber river.

Obedient as he was, Bruno immediately left the Chartreuse hermitage and travelled to Rome. The first Carthusians lost their courage quite easily without the spiritual example of their master. They spread out and left the Grande Chartreuse orphaned. Some months later most of the monks returned and they resumed their solitary life. Landuino was elected as the first successor of Bruno.

When Bruno arrived in Rome he was forced to escape with the Pope towards Mileto in Calabria. The city of Rome was occupied by the troops of the emperor and the antipope. The atmosphere in the upper echelons of the Church, however, had an unsettling effect on Bruno's mind. His only desire was the search for God in solitude and silence. He continuously begged the Pope to let him return to Chartreuse, but the Holy Father had other plans for his former master. He believed Bruno to be the best person to occupy the vacant archiepiscopal see of Reggio in Calabria. Bruno refused to accept this appointment and begged the

Pope once again to release him from this task. Finally the Pope allowed him to resume the solitary life. Pope Urban II made one condition, that Bruno settle in Italy.

The Prince of Calabria offered Bruno some territory near Reggio. And so, in the year 1091, the new Carthusian monastery of Santa Maria della Torre (Holy Lady of the Tower) was founded. Nowadays, this village is called Serra San Bruno. The settlement didn't have the same isolation and natural ruggedness as the Grande Chartreuse. The climate was much softer and the generous offerings of territories by local noble families became a real threat to the protection of the ideals of solitude and simplicity. When Prior Landuino visited Calabria in 1099, Bruno wrote a letter to his brothers in the Grande Chartreuse:

1. Brother Bruno, to his brethren in Christ, beloved more than anything in the world: greetings in the Lord.

    Through our dear brother Landuino's account, so detailed and so consoling, I have learned of your uncompromising yet wise observance, so commendable and deserving of praise. He spoke to me about your holy love, your untiring zeal for purity of heart and virtue. My spirit rejoices in the Lord. Yes, I rejoice, I give praise and thanks to the Lord, at the same time that I sigh with sorrow. I rejoice, yes – it is right that I should – to see you grow in virtue; but I am distressed and blush, being so sluggish and neglectful in the misery of my sins.

2. Rejoice, my dear brothers, over your blessed vocation and the generous gift of divine grace you have received. Rejoice over having escaped the turbulent waters

of this world, where there are so many perils and shipwrecks. Rejoice over having reached the peaceful quiet of a sheltered cove. Many desire to arrive there; many even tried to attain it, but did not arrive. Many did not remain after experiencing it, because they had not received that grace from God. Also, my brothers, take it as certain and proven: no one, after having enjoyed so desirable a good, can ever give it up without regrets, if he is serious about the salvation of his soul.

3. This I say about you, my beloved brothers: my soul glorifies the Lord, when I consider the wonders of his mercy toward you. After hearing the report of your dear Father Prior, who is filled with joy and pride because of you, I too rejoice because, even though you do not read, almighty God with his own finger has written love and the knowledge of his holy law in your hearts. By your works you show what you love and what you know. With all possible care and zeal you practise true obedience, which is doing the will of God, the key and the seal of all spiritual observance, and that could never be without great humility and outstanding patience accompanied by a chaste love for the Lord and true charity. It is clear that you are wisely reaping the sweet and refreshing fruits of the Divine Scriptures.

4. Therefore, my brothers, remain in the condition you are in, and flee as from a pestilence those deceitful laymen who seek to corrupt you, distributing their writings and whispering into your ear things that they neither understand nor love and which they contradict by their words and their acts. They are idle gyrovagues who

disgrace every good religious and think they should be praised for defaming those who really deserve praise, while they despise rules and obedience.

5. I would like to keep brother Landuino with me because he is often seriously ill. But because he feels he cannot find health, or joy, or life, or any improvement without you, he disagrees with me. His tears and sighs for your sake have shown me what you are to him and how much he loves all of you in perfect charity. I do not want to force him to stay, because I do not want to hurt him, or you, who are so dear to me on account of the merit of your virtues. That, my brothers, is why I urge you, I humbly but energetically beg you to show by your deeds the charity that you nourish in your hearts for him who is your beloved Father and Prior and tactfully and attentively provide for him whatever his numerous infirmities require. Perhaps he will decline to accept your loving services, preferring to endanger his health and his life rather than mitigate in any way the strictness of exterior observance, which of course could not be permitted; but that will no doubt be because he who is first in the community would blush to find himself last in observance and because he would fear to be the one among you to become lax and lukewarm on account of weakness. In my opinion, there is no reason to fear that. So that you will not be deprived of this grace, I authorise you to take my place in this one matter: you have permission to oblige him, respectfully, to take everything you give him for his health.

6. As regards myself, know that what I desire most after
    God is to go to see you. And as soon as I can, I will,
    with the help of God. Farewell.[32]

Bruno's letter to his Carthusian brothers is above all an
expression of joy and gratitude. The stories Landuino
told pleased him and made him happy. The monks in the
Grande Chartreuse did indeed adhere faithfully to their
monastic and solitary vocation. For Bruno it was proof
that God looked after his precarious project. Bruno's letter
also reveals his paternal concern and fraternal admonition.
He was truly concerned about Landuino's weak health
and about the immoral influences of the outside world. In
Bruno's concept of monastic life, discipline had to remain
human, reasonable and attainable. Perfection was not found
in excesses but rather in obedience, devotion and surrender.
The long and dangerous journey from Grenoble to Calabria
had exhausted and weakened Landuino. Bruno considered
his return both impossible and irresponsible. It would take
several weeks for Landuino to return home on horseback.
The privations he would suffer on the way could perhaps
be fatal.

When Landuino left Calabria, he was arrested near Rome
by the soldiers of Clement III, the antipope. Because he
refused to recognise Clement III as the true successor of St
Peter, the false pope locked Landuino in prison. A few days
after his release in September 1100 he died. Landuino is the
first martyr of the Carthusian order. The reason for his visit

---

[32]   Saint Bruno, *Letter to his Carthusian brothers* (www.chartreux.org).

to Bruno still remains unknown, similarly, it is not known how Bruno's letter finally reached the Grande Chartreuse.

It is relevant here to give a brief explanation concerning Bruno's warning in the address he made to the friars of the Grande Chartreuse. Bruno wrote in his letter that they were to avoid all influences of the so-called _gyrovagues_,[33] those itinerant monks who moved from village to village preaching in the valley of the Chartreuse massif. Their unsettled and seemingly agitated lifestyle might easily influence the simple minds of the illiterate friars. Bruno was concerned about them and so he warned them to be clear-headed and to stand firm against the lifestyle and message of these wandering preachers.

St Bruno

Completely exhausted, Bruno died in his monastery in Calabria on 6 October 1101 from causes unknown to present-day researchers. He was nearly 68 years old. According to tradition, prior to his death in the presence of all his assembled brothers, Bruno pronounced a trinitarian profession of faith.

1. I firmly believe in the Father, the Son, and the Holy Spirit: the Father unbegotten, the only begotten Son, the Holy Spirit proceeding from them both; and I believe that these three Persons are but one God.

---

[33] _Gyrovagues_: itinerant or wandering monks. Composition from the Greek word _gyro_ (circle) and the Latin word _vagus_ (wandering).

2. I believe that the same Son of God was conceived
by the Holy Spirit in the womb of the Virgin Mary. I
believe that the Virgin was chaste before she bore her
child, that she remained a virgin while she bore her
child, and continued a virgin ever after. I believe that
the same Son of God was conceived among men, a
true man with no sin. I believe the same Son of God
was captured by the hatred of some of the Jews who
did not believe, was bound unjustly, covered with
spittle, and scourged. I believe that he died, was buried,
and descended into hell to free those of his who were
held there. He descended for our redemption, he rose
again, he ascended into heaven, and from there he will
come to judge the living and the dead.

3. I believe also in the sacraments that the Church believes
and holds in reverence, and especially that what has
been consecrated on the altar is the true Flesh and the
true Blood of our Lord Jesus Christ, which we receive
for the forgiveness of our sins and in the hope of
eternal salvation. I believe in the resurrection of the
flesh and everlasting life.

4. I acknowledge and believe the holy and ineffable
Trinity, Father, Son, and Holy Spirit, to be but only
one God, of only one substance, of only one nature,
of only one majesty and power. We profess that the
Father was neither begotten nor created but that he has
begotten. The Father takes his origin from no one; of
him the Son is born and the Holy Spirit proceeds. He
is the source and origin of all Divinity. And the Father,
ineffable by his very nature, from his own substance
has begotten the Son ineffably; but he has begotten

nothing except what he is himself: God has begotten God, light has begotten light, and it is from him that all Fatherhood in heaven and on earth proceeds. Amen.[34]

Bruno's profession of faith had been forgotten for many years, until it was coincidentally discovered in the sixteenth century in the archives of the Carthusian monastery in Calabria. 'Bruno's profession of faith is the expression of a real contemplative soul. The text completes our limited knowledge of Bruno's desire alongside what we read in his letters. It reveals his most intimate dreams about a solitary life in the desert. With admiration and love he contemplated the four most important mysteries of Christian faith: the mysteries of the Father, the Eucharist, the Incarnation and the Passion, along with the mystery of Mary, Mother and Virgin. These four mysteries were the true fundamentals of his life of joy. At his last breath he turned his eyes towards the treasures of Revelation. His lips expressed his raison d'être. Bruno's profession of faith is a declaration of love. He desired to die in the divine Light that had enlightened him during his life on earth.'[35]

After Bruno's death, the Carthusians of Calabria sent a message of condolence to all monasteries and dioceses who had known him. This parchment scroll, called *Tituli Funebres*, contains at least 178 condolences and prayers. The chronology of these condolences reveals more or less the journey of the messenger who carried it. He left Calabria

---

[34]   Saint Bruno, *Profession of faith* (www.chartreux.org).
[35]   A. Ravier, *Saint Bruno*, pp. 213–14.

via Tuscany towards the north of Italy, he passed the Alps towards Grenoble and the Grande Chartreuse. He continued his itinerary along some famous French abbeys like Cluny, Cîteaux and Molesmes. The messenger called at Paris and Reims and then reached Germany, then Flanders and even England. It is quite astonishing that no trace of Bruno's native city, namely Cologne, is perceived on the death roll. Probably different parts have been lost or rotted throughout time. The monks of the Grande Chartreuse wrote this beautiful funeral oration: 'We, the brothers of Chartreuse, are more than sad because the death of our beloved and famous father Bruno deprives us of consolation. We are prepared to do everything that benefits his holy and dear soul. But the graces we owe him will tell us what we have to do. From now on and forever we will pray for our unique father and master. We shall celebrate Masses and we shall pray for him as we use to do for all deceased, as it fits good children.'[36]

Bruno's body was buried in the monastery cemetery in Calabria, but later his relics were kept in the church, where they remain to this day. Like the Trappist monks, the Carthusians preserve the custom of burying their deceased without a coffin directly in the naked earth. The dead body is laid down on a stretcher and the cap is pulled over the head and seamed. A remarkable custom in the Carthusian order is the use of anonymous graves: no names are written on the crosses. Eternal life is indeed the ultimate goal of a Carthusian monk. Only the tombs of the priors of the

---

[36]   A. Ravier, *Saint Bruno*, pp. 215.

Grande Chartreuse have stone crosses engraved with their
names. Because most graves are reused after a couple of years,
a Carthusian cemetery can count hundreds of dead bodies.
'Carthusian graveyards are quite impressive,' witnesses
Cardinal Danneels. 'There are merely simple wooden
crosses without any names. No decorations, no pictures,
no tombstones, sometimes even no maintenance. It is really
significant for the Carthusian way of life: simplicity and
humility. Monks are like candles: they just burn for God.'[37]
In Guigo's *Customs of Chartreuse* we can read more about the
ancient Carthusian death rituals: 'The deceased is washed
and dressed, a monk in his penitential robe with stockings
and shoes; a friar in his habit and cap with stockings and
shoes. The body is placed on a stretcher and carried into
the church. If there is still enough time the funeral will take
place on the same day, but always after Mass has been sung
for the deceased. If there is not enough time, the funeral
will take place the next day. Monks and friars pray during
the night in presence of the body ... The next day, after
the Convent Mass has been sung, the funeral will take place
in this manner: the community gathers around the dead
body and the priest prays the *Pater Noster* ... The deceased
is carried to the grave while psalms are prayed. When they
arrive at the grave the priest prays the *Pater Noster* ... He
blesses the pit with holy water and incense. Then the body is
laid down into the pit. While the body is covered with earth,
psalms are sang and the priest prays *Obsceramus*.'[38]

---

[37]   M. De Roeck, *Kardinaal Danneels over Into Great Silence*, p. 1.
[38]   *Customs of Chartreuse*, 13, 3–8.

Bruno was canonised in 1514 by Pope Leo X (1513–21). In 1623 his universal worship was approved by Pope Gregory XV (1621–23). Compared with other founders of religious orders (for example Sts Bernard, Francis or Dominic), Bruno's canonisation took a long time. Even Bishop Hugo from Grenoble was canonised two years after his death. 'The Carthusian order has never been eager to have its members, even those of manifest holiness, canonised. "Be a saint rather than be called one", as the Carthusians used to say. The hidden life continues even after death.'[39] The memorial feast of St Bruno takes place on 6 October.

St Bruno has never been a popular saint, except in a few villages in the Chartreuse massif and Calabria, the home of the first Carthusian foundation. Twice a year, at Pentecost and on 6 October, a solemn procession is organised by the local parish of Serra San Bruno. The procession begins at the gate of the Carthusian monastery. The ancient golden bust with a piece of Bruno's skull is carried by the faithful through all the streets and squares of the village. With great care the monks entrust the precious reliquary to the huge crowd of pilgrims. The highlight of the feast is the nocturnal vigil culminating in the Eucharist in the parish church. Pilgrims come to pray and to receive blessings and absolution. People throw confetti, flowers and coins and they overload Bruno's statue with offerings and gifts. (That's why the statue is protected with a plastic cover.) A particular custom of popular devotion is the so-called *certosinetti* or 'Carthusian babies'. Newborn children are dressed in small

---

[39]   Charterhouse of the Transfiguration, *Carthusian Saints*, 2006, p. 5.

Carthusian habits and brought to the outer church of the
monastery where the prior blesses them all. In former
times St Bruno was invoked in this region as a protection
against demonic possession and insanity. His name is also
eponymous with San Bruno Creek in California.

A real iconography of St Bruno only emerges from the
middle of the fourteenth century. He is usually represented
in prayer, or with his forefinger on his lips as a sign of
the silence of the Carthusian order. The skull he holds
symbolises his withdrawal to the desert. The staff and mitre
at his feet refer to the symbols of Bruno's refusal of the
episcopate. In the Basilica of St Peter in Rome, Bruno is
represented in this way. His statue is placed among the other
founders of religious orders.

On the occasion of the nine hundredth anniversary of
the death of St Bruno in 2001, Pope John Paul II (1978–
2005) wrote a message to all members of the Carthusian
order. He gave thanks for their prayer and witness and he
encouraged them in their vocation and charism. In October
1984 Pope John Paul II visited the Carthusian community
in Serra San Bruno and prayed at Bruno's reliquary, just
as Pope Benedict XVI did on 9 October 2011. We offer
some of the beautiful passages out of the papal letter to the
Carthusians:

> At the time when the members of the Carthusian
> family celebrate the ninth centenary of their Founder's
> death, I, with them, give thanks to God who raised up
> in His Church the eminent and ever topical figure of St
> Bruno. Praying fervently I appreciate your witness of
> faithfulness to the see of Peter and am happy to join in

with the joy of the Carthusian Order which has in this good and incomparable father a master of the spiritual life. On October 6, 1101, Bruno, aflame with divine love left the elusive shadows of this world to join the everlasting goods for ever (Cf. *Letter to Ralph*, 13). The brothers of the hermitage of Santa Maria della Torre in Calabria little knew that this *dies natalis* inaugurated a singular spiritual venture which even today brings forth abundant fruits for the Church and the world.

Bruno witnessed the cultural and religious upheavals of his time, in a Europe that was taking shape. He was an actor in the reform, which the Church, faced with internal difficulties, wished to fulfil. After having been an appreciated teacher he felt called to consecrate himself to that unique Good which God is. 'What is there as good as God? Better still, is there another Good than God alone? Really, a holy soul who has any sense of this Good, of its incomparable splendour and beauty, finds himself aflame with heavenly love and exclaims: 'I am thirsting for the strong and living God; when shall I go and see the face of God?' (*Letter to Ralph,* 15). The uncompromising nature of that thirst drove Bruno, a patient listener to the Spirit, to invent with his first companions a style of eremitical life where everything favours one's response to the call from Christ — who indeed ever chooses men to lead them into solitude and join themselves to Him in intimate love. By this choice of life in the desert, Bruno invites the entire Church community never to lose sight of the highest vocation which is to remain forever with the Lord ... To a father's vigour he joined the sensitivity of a mother. These exquisite remarks from the obituary scroll show the fruitfulness of a life given to contemplate the face of Christ as the source of all apostolic fecundity and brotherly love. Would that St Bruno's sons and daughters, as did their father, may always keep on contemplating Christ, that they 'keep watch in this way for the return of their Master ever ready to open when He knocks' (*Letter to Ralph*, 4); this will be a stimulant call for all Christians to stay vigilant in prayer in order to welcome their Lord! ... The call to prayer and contemplation, which is the hallmark of Carthusian life, shows particularly that only Christ can bring to the hopes of men a fullness of meaning and joy ...

The ninth centenary of St Bruno's *dies natalis* gives me the occasion to renew my trust in the Carthusian Order, in its mission of selfless contemplation and intercession for the Church and the world. Following St Bruno and his successors, the Carthusian monasteries never stop awakening the Church to the eschatological dimension of its mission, calling to mind God's marvellous deeds and being watchful in the expectation of the ultimate accomplishment of the virtue of Hope (Cf. *Vita Consecrata*, § 27). Watching tirelessly for the Kingdom to come, seeking to Be rather than to Do, the Carthusian Order gives the Church vigour and courage in its mission to put out in deep waters and permit the Good News of Christ to enkindle all of mankind.

In these days of Carthusian celebration I ardently pray the Lord to make resound in the heart of many young, the call to leave everything to follow the poor man Christ, on the demanding but liberating path of the Carthusian vocation. I also invite those in charge of the Carthusian family to respond without timidity to the requests from the young Churches to found monasteries on their territories.

In this spirit the discernment and formation of the candidates presenting themselves necessitates renewed attention from the novice masters. Indeed today's culture marked by strong hedonistic currents, by the wish for possessions and a certain wrong conception of freedom, does not make it easy for the young to express their generosity, when they want to consecrate their lives to Christ, to follow him on the path of self-offering love, of concrete and generous service. The complexity of each one's itinerary, their psychological fragility, the difficulties to live faithfully over the years, all this suggests that nothing must be neglected in giving those who ask for admission to the Carthusian desert a formation spanning all the dimensions of the human person. What is more, particular attention must be given to the choice of educators able to accompany candidates on the paths of interior liberation and docility to the Holy Spirit. Finally, aware that life together as brothers is a fundamental element of the itinerary of consecrated persons, communities must be invited to live unreservedly their mutual love, and develop a spiritual climate and lifestyle in conformity with your Order's charisma …

It is up to you, dear sons and daughters of the Charterhouse, heirs to St Bruno's charisma, to maintain in all its authenticity and depth the specific spiritual path, which he traced for you by his words and example. Your pithy knowledge of God, matured in prayer and meditation of His word, calls the people of God to look further, to the very horizons of a renewed humankind inquest of fullness of meaning and unity … Your hidden life with Christ, as the Cross silently planted in the heart of redeemed mankind, remains in fact for the Church and for the world the eloquent sign and the permanent reminder that anybody, yesterday as today, can let himself be taken by Him who is only love.[40]

On 3 June 2014, on the occasion of the fifth centenary of the so-called canonisation of St Bruno, Pope Francis also addressed his admiration to the members of the Carthusian order in a papal message and blessing.[41]

---

[40] Message of Pope John Paul II for the ninth centenary of St Bruno's death, 14 May 2001.
[41] Cf. Message of Pope Francis for the fifth centenary of St Bruno's canonisation, 3 June 2014.

2

The Rule of the Carthusian Order

The originality of St Bruno's concept

St Bruno was certainly no 'unicorn' in his time. The eleventh
and twelfth centuries were a flourishing period for monastic
life. Cluny Abbey was still expanding and also the Cistercian
order had a burning and attractive charisma. Likewise many
men and women felt called to the ancient ideal of the
Desert Fathers. Solitary life indeed was considered as a stage
of spiritual perfection. Solitary monks – who lived literally
monos, or alone, according to the Greek word – could live
undisturbed in prayer and contemplation.

The most successful experiment in the solitary life prior
to Bruno was obviously that of St Romuald (d. 1027), who
founded the Camaldolese order in the beginning of the
eleventh century. In Camaldoli, situated in the Apennine
Mountains of Tuscany, he developed a concept of a
double monastery in which a small community of hermits
in the high mountains was protected by a community of
Benedictine monks deeper in the valley. So the unique
combination of coenobitic and anchoretic monasticism

appeared for the first time in Camaldoli: a combination of a monastic life in community (coenobitic life) and a monastic life in solitude (anchoretic life).[42] This unique combination of monastic lifestyles took a totally different form within the Carthusian order, as we shall see.

During the High Middle Ages innumerable new attempts at eremitic life sprang up on Western European soil. Some hermits drew back into the mountains or into the forests, others to an island or a cave. Some lived in the vicinity of an abbey or a parish church, while others wandered as penitential preachers or beggars. In short, the history of monastic, solitary life contains very radical forms of solitude and asceticism. The most extreme are of course the stylites and recluses. The stylites or pillar-saints, who lived mostly between the fifth and the nineteenth centuries in the Eastern Churches, sometimes sat or stood for many years on a pillar several feet high in order to separate themselves from society. The most famous among these solitary fakirs is Simeon the Elder, who sat for more than 36 years on a

---

[42]   The Camaldolese order celebrates its first millennium in 2012–13. According to the ancient sources, the foundation of Camaldoli dates from the year 1012, however other sources point out later dates. In the sixteenth century the Camaldolese order split into two different branches: Paulus Giustiniani returned radically to the first love of his spiritual father Romuald, namely solitary life. Nowadays the Camaldolese order still has two branches: the Benedictine Camaldolese monks who are a part of the Confederation of the Benedictine order (there is also a female branch) and the Camaldolese hermits of Monte Corona. Both have monasteries in the USA (Big Sur, California and Bloomingdale, Ohio). During spring 2012, the Camaldolese hermits of Monte Corona offered us an exceptional opportunity to participate in their lives and to stay in a real hermitage in the monastery of Monte Rua near Padua (Italy). A special word of thanks to Dom Winfrido, the prior of the small community of anchorites. Cf. T. Peeters, 'Dossier: Duizend jaar Camaldoli', *Tertio* 644 (13 June 2012), pp. 8–9.

high pillar in the Syrian desert! The only known case of 'pillar holiness' in the Western Church is the deacon Walfroy, who climbed to the top of his pillar at the end of the sixth century in the French Ardennes, not far from the Belgian border and near the famous Orval Abbey. According to a legend he literally froze on his pillar during a severe winter!

The recluses on the other hand let themselves be locked up or immured alive in a dungeon or a crypt. Their spiritual example par excellence is St Antony Abbot, who withdrew in the fourth century to a crypt in an Egyptian necropolis. In recluse spirituality, a solitary cell is symbolic of a grave or a dungeon in which one is buried alive, forgotten by society and dead in the eyes of the world. One of the most famous recluses is St Colette, the reformer of the Claris nuns. In the fifteenth century she was immured against a wall in the church of Corbie in the north of France. But even far into the twentieth century, traces are found of this extraordinary and strange form of solitary life: in 1945, Sr Maria Nazarena, the famous Camaldolese anchoress born in the USA (Connecticut), withdrew to a small room in the St Anthony's convent on the Aventine Hill in Rome. She lived in complete isolation for more than 45 years until she died in 1990, aged 82. She only left her cell twice: for visits to an oculist and a dentist.[43] Both Pope Paul VI and Pope

---

[43]　The Camaldolese order, both male as well as the female branch, is the only monastic order in the Catholic world which offers the possibility of total reclusion. Recluses never leave their cells, unless in exceptional circumstances or on special occasions like Easter Sunday. In 2009, Dom Gianmaria from Tokyo died in the Camaldolese Hermitage of Monte Rua after 16 years of total reclusion and isolation. The only recluse monk for the moment is Dom Nicolas of Puerto Rico, who lives in the Camaldolese Hermitage of Bloomingdale (Ohio, USA). Some years ago, a new anchoress with-

John Paul II visited Sr Nazarena during their pontificate. On 21 November 2013, Pope Francis visited the monastery of the Camaldolese nuns on the Aventine Hill as well as the recluse cell of Sr Nazarena.[44]

Because solitude is the purpose of a reclusive life, it is quite obvious that some asked Carthusian monks to be their spiritual pen pals. Bernard, the first prior of the Carthusian monastery of Portes (near Lyon), and Denys the Carthusian (d. 1471), the famous so-called *doctor extaticus*, or the 'ecstatic teacher', from the Charterhouse in Roermond (Holland), accomplished this task as spiritual guide of several recluse hermits. Both wrote letters about the monastic ideal of solitary life. We reproduce some of the most interesting parts on solitude, silence and contemplation. The letter of Prior Bernard to the recluse hermit Raynaud, written in the beginning of the twelfth century, is one of the most ancient writings within the Carthusian tradition:

> Let's talk about silence in the first place. I think you must preserve absolute silence after Compline until Prime the next morning during summer and until Terce during winter. Whenever circumstances allow, you must constantly seek to preserve silence. Especially during the night, silence must be preserved unless some necessity forces an interruption. In that case be

drew in the Camaldolese monastery on the Aventine Hill in Rome. Cf. T. Peeters, 'Milles ans sont comme un jour. Les camaldules fêtent leur millénaire', *Collectanea Cisterciensia* (74/2012/3), pp. 305–12.

[44]   Cf. *Address of Pope Francis to the Camaldolese Benedictine Nuns*, 21 November 2013.

circumspect and reserved in what you say. Never use empty and useless words and don't listen when others do so. Never be seduced to participate in worldly chats, jokes or gossip. Be selective when you hear news: only listen to those pieces which invite you to praise God's wonders; or to sad and terrible news which invites you to implore God's blessings. Whenever you receive visitors, only speak good words. If you receive clerics or intellectuals, listen rather than speak. If you follow this advice, no worldly vanity will disturb your inner peace during psalmody and prayer. It is your duty to adhere to this advice, because it is written in Holy Scriptures. The Lord says in the Gospel: 'But I tell you that everyone will have to give account on the day of judgement for every empty word they have spoken' (Matt. 12:36). Further it is written: 'Sin is not ended by multiplying words' (Prov. 10:19) … And also this: 'Death and life are in the power of the tongue' (Prov. 18:21). Therefore accomplish the content of this psalm you always pray: 'I said, I will take heed to my ways, that I sin not with my tongue: I will keep my mouth with a bridle, while the wicked is before me' (Ps. 39:1–3). In this psalm is also written: 'I was dumb with silence, I held my peace, *even* from good.' When the prophet says that it is better to be silent about good things, so all the more about bad things! …

About prayer: remember that you must pray incessantly. Pray with greatest care. No sorrow or illness may restrain you from praying. Don't pray merely for your own salvation, but for the salvation of all faithful: for the deceased and for the unborn and

especially for those who help you and also for us. Trust
on the guidance of the Holy Spirit who, according to
the word of the Lord, will teach the saints how to pray
with inexpressible lamentations. Enter into the temple
of your heart, close the door from all vanities, impure
thoughts and seductions of the enemy and pray to your
Father who is present in secret. Try to take care about
your inner life with greatest devotion according to
your capacities and the grace of God. Take advantage
of these moments!

The care for holy meditation: beside psalmody and
prayer you must meditate on God's Law, especially
during morning hours because these are the most
merciful moments of the day. Meditate in the silence
of your heart on God's will for you and how it can
be accomplished. Try to direct the spirit of your
heart and action towards the divine commandments
and the example of the ancient Fathers. Always keep
this biblical verse in mind: 'Above all else, guard your
heart, for everything you do flows from it' (Prov. 4:23).
Human spirit is weak. Therefore you must direct your
spirit with great care towards holy meditation. Then
you won't be seduced by vain and impure thoughts
which are inaccessibly suggested and whispered by the
enemy. When this happens, your spirit won't be able to
pray any more.[45]

[45]   Bernard de Portes, 'Lettre au reclus Raynaud', in *Lettres des premiers chartreux* (SC 274), pp. 53, 65, 67.

The letter of Denys the Carthusian about recluse solitary life is a practical manual or rule for the daily routine of the recluse anchoress:

> A life of separation, loneliness and confinement has not only a future goal, that is bliss in heaven, but also a secular goal, which is Love! Charity is the most important virtue, that's why all Christians have to direct their virtuous acts towards the love of God. Many external activities and all sorts of efforts prevent a permanent direction to God, and even so do storms of desires, pursuit of vanity, personal problems and other worries. The more man can deliver himself from these thoughts, the more he will be able to cherish God with eager and tender love. A concentrated force is much more effective than a divided one and the human heart is much more alive when it is directed towards just one single love than when it is confused by several ones.
>
> A recluse has to deliver from all things which impede the love of God. How more able she is to renounce, to abstain and to refuse. How stronger she will be to devote on a pure, lasting, free and eager love for the Lord. The love of God is the only goal of her life, is it not? This is the secret of a recluse and solitary life on earth. Day by day she must open her heart completely for this divine love. Without this goal it is totally useless and absurd to lock yourself in a cell or a dungeon ...
>
> If it is true that an eager, tender and sweet love for God is the ultimate goal of confinement, then

it is also true that an authentic, elevated and lasting contemplation of God – as far as possible on earth – is the ultimate goal of solitary life. The one cannot exist without the other. How more the recluse proceeds in her love for God, how wiser she will become and how better she will contemplate! ... So the recluse knows what she must do and how she must order her activities. She knows which goal she has to reach, to await and to desire ...

Aristotle, the most intelligent among the pagans, once said: 'A solitaire is a beast or a god.' Indeed, man is a social being and solitary life is not a natural gift. But when a recluse tries to live according to the requirements of a cell, she will surpass human nature and she will reach God. Brave men often are called lions and greedy men wolves, because their behaviour is similar to these animals. A contemplative person is called a divine person, because he knows how to intimate the characteristics and the actions of God's own life ...

The solitary cell is fitted up in a way that the recluse can only conduct divine activities in it: contemplation, love, compassion for the world, kindness for all creatures. All these virtuous acts will please God. But above all it is God who grants faith, hope, contemplation, prayer, praise and perseverance. That's why the recluse is able to abandon self to the contemplation of God, the fear of God, eager love, joyful prayer, singing, praising and interceding for humanity, especially for the sinners. But this is the most important duty of a recluse: unity with God, as far as human weakness allows. During all activities, on each moment and on each place – if she eats, drinks or whatever she does – the recluse must try to keep unity with God … Do not think this is impossible! Whoever is gripped and possessed by human love shall feel united with his beloved, wherever he is, whatever he does and on each moment. God, who is the pure and infinite good, is the most desirable and elevated desire of us all, isn't it? … The recluse who fills her days with virtue, contemplation, prayer, heavenly desire and love for eternity, will never be exhausted, but she will be fulfilled by happiness. When she is able to endure in love and progress, she will be very happy. It is like St Bernard says: solitaries remain in their cells like angels in heaven, and permanently they soar from their cells on earth to their dwellings in heaven.[46]

Most attempts at solitary life in the age of St Bruno had to deal with the same problem. The number of followers became too numerous and therefore the necessity of a rule became urgent. Most hermits returned to coenobitic life and joined the Benedictine or the Cistercian order or a community of regular canons.

Most monastic experiments in the eleventh and twelfth centuries successively abandoned the element of solitude to proceed into a new, organised form of community life. Generally silence received an important place, but solitude did not. The moments of

---

46   Denys le Chartreux, *Livre de vie des recluses* (*Spir. Cart.*), pp. 28–9, 36–7.

silence were limited in time, but not in space. In other words: monks and cloistered nuns weren't physically alone, they were at best 'to be to their selves' in certain moments which were devoted to silence, study and personal prayer. And most often these silent moments were organised in common places and in community. In comparison with most other monastic traditions, the Carthusian order gave a dominant role to solitude. The Carthusians did not only measure the moments 'to be to their selves', they are in fact most of the time physically alone. Within the spectrum of Western monastic families, the Carthusian tradition is the most anchoretic. Within the colourful world of hermits, the Carthusian tradition is the most organised form of solitary life. Georges Duby once called the Carthusian life the less anarchic form of the widespread endeavour for solitude in Bruno's age.[47]

The originality of St Bruno exists in the concept of a *modus vivendi* for a community of hermits with a perfect harmony between coenobitic and anchoretic monasticism. His approach was fundamentally different from the concept of St Romuald in Camaldoli, because the Camaldolese order contained coenobites. A Carthusian monastery is a community of hermits – anchorites – who share a minimal form of community life. This principle applies also to the converses: they are not coenobitic monks but real hermits, because they also share a minimal form of community

---

[47]   P. Nissen, *Eenzaamheid als zoeken naar God*, pp. 96–7.

life. 'Bruno innovated and created, not by establishing a total new practice, but by uniting very ancient monastic concepts: separation from the world, long moments of prayer, especially during the night, *lectio divina*, silence, fasting and manual labour were practised by the Desert Fathers and they are found in all monastic rules. But Bruno subdivided all these elements in a new order, introducing also new accents.'[48] We may assume that Bruno was very familiar with the writings of the ancient Fathers, the desert monks and the broad monastic tradition. Above all, he was a famous theologian and lived for more than two years in the shadow of the Benedictine abbey of Molesmes. 'It is quite remarkable to notice the almost identical wording of the Carthusian and the Benedictine profession formula: only the phrase 'according to the Rule of St Benedict' is cancelled. Obviously Bruno did not intend a *familia* of brothers gathered around the person of the *pater familias* (father of the family) or the abbot, but a community of true blood hermits.'[49]

However, Bruno had no intention of instituting a new monastic order. He is without question the founder of the Carthusians, but he left no written rule for his followers. His example and his teachings were a kind of living rule for them. In Calabria, Bruno established an identical copy of

---

[48] M. Theeuwes, *Bruno van Keulen*, p. 106.

[49] T. Peeters, 'L'Ordre des Chartreux et le monachisme bénédictin: une branche au meme tronc?', *Collectanea Cisterciensia* (72/2010/3), p. 323. Cf. N. Nabert, 'Rites et paroles de la profession solennelle dans l'Ordre des Chartreux', in R. Bindel (red.), *35 Années de recherché et de spiritualité. Congrès International des Analecta Cartusiana du 23 au 26 juin 2005, Chartreuse de Molsheim – France* (AC 253), pp. 11–21.

the monastic concept he established once in the Chartreuse massif. His brothers preserved Bruno's orders with great care and they passed them over to their successors. Some 30 years later, somewhere between 1121 and 1128, Prior Guigo I wrote down the customs of the first Carthusian monks in the *Consuetudines Cartusiae* or *The Customs of Chartreuse*.[50]

We may conclude by assuming that it was impossible for St Bruno to impose the existing monastic rule on the Carthusian concept. The combination he made of the anchoretic and coenobitic monasticism into one single community of hermit monks was really new in the Middle Ages. Each practice he borrowed from other monastic traditions was profoundly transformed in the grounding of solitary life. 'Because of his deepest aspirations, Bruno offered a very free opposite to Western monasticism without force. He merely arranged existing traditions in a new manner. It reveals his inner desires, his very personal and well-considered call, which was indeed so personal that it was impossible to adapt any existing rule.'[51]

Guigo I and The Customs of Chartreuse

'We cannot underestimate the priceless contribution of Guigo I (1083–1136) in the design and the development of the Carthusian order. By writing down *The Customs of*

---

[50] According to the study of Dom Maurice Laporte, the famous historian of the Carthusian order, the most plausible date of the redaction is between the end of 1127 and the beginning of 1128. Cf. M. Laporte, *Aux sources de la vie cartusienne* 2, 1960–71, pp. 58–62.

[51] M. Theeuwes, *Bruno van Keulen*, p. 106.

Chartreuse, he made Bruno's dream – and therefore the dream of all Carthusian monks and nuns throughout the ages – real. Indeed, Guigo rendered a strong stability and durability to the young and fragile start of the Carthusian concept. Not only through conservation, but also through innovation and creation. In other words, he gave the primitive Carthusian community its juridical foundation."[52] In order to survive, each form of religious life needs a certain order, stability, legislation and authority. Very precisely and extremely detailed, Guigo I wrote down all aspects of daily Carthusian life in the form of a monastic rule. The Carthusians accept *The Customs of Chartreuse* 'as [if] it were sparks of light thrown off from the soul of him, to whom the Holy Spirit entrusted the compilation of the first laws of our Order.'[53]

Guigo I is the youngest prior in the history of the Carthusian order: in 1109 he was elected as the fifth successor of St Bruno, at the age of 26. During his governance, at least seven new monasteries were founded, including the Charterhouse of Portes (1115), where today a very vital community continues to live. In 1132, Guigo I had to face the terrible avalanche which destroyed the original settlement of Bruno and killed most of the monks. He took the decision to build a new monastery down in the valley, precisely on the spot where the actual monastery of the Grande Chartreuse is situated. Besides *The Customs*

---

[52] T. Peeters, 'Inleiding', in Guigo de Kartuizer, *Gewoonten. Een leefregel voor kluizenaars in gemeenschap*, p. 54.

[53] Prologue to the statutes of the Carthusian order, 2.1.

of Chartreuse, Guigo I left us a few letters and two other interesting writings: a *Biography of Bishop Hugo from Grenoble* and the so-called *Meditations*, in which he wrote down his experiences and concerns as prior. The last years of his life were spent bearing great illness. Guigo I died at the age of 53.

The Customs of Chartreuse are a very faithful reproduction of the original lifestyle of the Carthusian pioneers, because some of the first companions of St Bruno were still alive when the redaction took place. The book contains all manner of directions about daily life in a hermit cell; about the Carthusian liturgy; about the observations regarding fasting and poverty; and about the different tasks and responsibilities within the community. But Guigo I also introduced certain changes and innovations into the existing tradition. The *numerus clausus* of 13 monks and 16 converses, or the increment of the minimum age of new candidates, and the restriction of the property rights of the community, are some examples. These reforms were not violations of the young tradition, but merely a protection to avoid repetition of certain problems or incidents in the future. *The Customs of Chartreuse* were written at the explicit request of Bishop Hugo from Grenoble in conjunction with some of the priors of the neighbouring monasteries. Bishop Hugo understood very well that only a written Code would make possible the successful implementation of the original observances in all new foundations. In the Prologue of *The Customs of Chartreuse*, Guigo I justified his writing:

'Obedient to the desire and counsel of our beloved and Reverend Father Hugo, the Bishop of Grenoble, to whom we cannot refuse anything, and also because of your repeated requests, we will hand over and write down the customs of our house. For different reasons we were unable to start earlier at this job. We are convinced that all our customs are based on the monastic customs of St Jerome, the Rule of St Benedict and other authentic writings. Besides – because of our vocation – we think it is much more useful for us to be instructed rather than to instruct, and to praise the merits of others rather than our own. Scripture says: 'Let someone else praise you, not your own mouth; a stranger, not your own lips.' As the Lord commands in the Gospel: 'Beware of practising your righteousness before men to be noticed by them; otherwise you have no reward with your Father who is in heaven' (Matt. 6:1). With the help of God we will explain how the Lord provides for us in this place, because we cannot resist your supplies and the authority and friendship of certain persons.'[54]After Guigo's death *The Customs of Chartreuse* were divided into chapters, titles and numbers and they received the form of a clear juridical code, which was later approved by Rome as the official Rule of the Carthusian order. Throughout history these statutes have been revised several times according to particular needs, for example the liturgical reforms of the Second Vatican Council (1962–65) and the promulgation of the new Code of Canon Law (1983). However, the Carthusians always remained faithful to the ancient ideal of their founder and to the spirit of Guigo's writing. More significantly, 'all general chapters bear witness to a radical return to the primitive sources of Chartreuse. *The Book*

---

[54]   Prologue of *The Customs of Chartreuse*.

of Customs was written for a community of only thirteen
monks and sixteen friars. The ancient principles had to be
adapted over and over again in each new monastery that
was founded in whatever Christian country of Western
Europe. It is quite obvious that some new monasteries
lost almost all resemblance to the beauty and solitude of
the high mountains and forest in the Chartreuse massif.'[55]
With some exaggeration the old aphorism *Cartusia numquam
reformata, quia numquam deformata* ('The Carthusian order was
never reformed because it was never deformed') remains
true even today. In his famous *Golden Epistle* to the newly
established Carthusian monastery of Mont-Dieu (French
Ardennes), the Cistercian William of St Thierry (d. 1148),
one of the greatest medieval spiritual writers, expressed his
understanding of certain changes: 'Your successors will call
you fathers and founders and they will grant you due respect
and imitation. Everything that you have decided, everything
that you have maintained and observed, and everything
that you have in custom, must be maintained and observed
by your successors without any change! No one has the
right to change anything ... And if something has to be
changed, God shall reveal what to do. Despite our respect
for the Carthusian holiness ... we agree that indeed some
observations are necessary in the bleak and cold Alps, but
not in other regions.'[56]

---

[55]   D. Le Blevec, 'Un érémitisme tempéré', *La Voie cartusienne. Une vie cachée en Dieu* (Car-
      mel, 107/2003), p. 16.
[56]   William of St Thierry, *Golden Epistle*, 22.

The government of the Carthusian order

Since the first general chapter in 1140, the supreme authority of the Carthusian order rests with the general chapter itself. Each two years, all the priors of the different monasteries gather in the Grande Chartreuse for a general assembly. Eight other monks are chosen by them to constitute the so-called *definitorium*, which holds all legislative and executive power. Between two general chapters, the prior general holds all rights and powers which are needed to rule the entire order. The prior general, who is called 'Reverend Father', is the *primus inter pares* among the other priors, so the first among equals.[57] That is why he does not receive the title of abbot, nor does he wear the insignias of a mitre, ring or pectoral cross. 'A mitred abbot is a public figure in the ecclesiastical world, but a Carthusian is made for solitude and secrecy.'[58] Or as Guigo I says, 'You are not made to be seen, to be known, to be loved, to be admired or to be adored, but to see, to know, to love, to admire and to adore the Lord. This is all that is useful for you, all the else is not.'[59] In each monastery a vicar (the right hand of the prior), a procurator or an economist, a spiritual adviser and a novice master is nominated to assist the prior in the daily governance of the community.

An important element in the government of the Carthusian order is the two-year visitation of all monasteries by two monks in order to guarantee discipline and

---

[57] See p. 15
[58] R. Serrou, *Au désert de Chartreuse. La vie solitaire des fils de Saint Bruno*, p. 62.
[59] *Meditations*, 288.

observance. Also the monasteries of the Carthusian nuns are inspected every two years by two monks.

The Carthusian nuns

In 1145 the abbey of Benedictine nuns in Prébayon (French Provence) decided to adapt *The Customs of Chartreuse* and the Carthusian observances. Since then, the Carthusian nuns have been accepted as the female branch of the order and they fall under the governance of the Prior General of the Grande Chartreuse. The sisters have their own general chapter, which includes the prior general, all the prioresses of the different monasteries, the inspectors and a few sisters. There are only five female Carthusian monasteries in the world: two in France, one in Italy, one in Spain and one in South Korea.[60]

For many centuries, the Carthusian nuns did not live according to the same regime of solitude and asceticism as the monks did. In fact, most general chapters were convinced that female psychology demands certain concessions. Therefore the sisters took their daily meals in community and they had more moments of common recreation. Only in 1970, on the explicit demand of the greatest part of the Carthusian nuns, the general chapter agreed to radicalise the regime of solitude and asceticism in all female monasteries. Today, monks and nuns live the same monastic ideal in its thoroughness.

---

[60] An interesting book with beautiful pictures about the life of the Carthusian nuns was published by N. Nabert, *Les moniales chartreuses*, Ad Solem, 2009.

Just as the monks, so too the Carthusian nuns hold the difference between the cloistered sisters on the one hand and the converse and donate sisters on the other. The cloistered nuns devote their lives to silent prayer and labour in their solitary cells, while the converse and donate sisters are responsible for all material cares in the monastery. If they desire it, the cloistered nuns may receive virginal consecration after they pronounce their perpetual vows. A ring and a veil symbolise their mystic marriage with Christ. Particular to the Carthusian order is the remarkable fact that these consecrated virgins may wear the stole of a deacon during the liturgy, in particular to read the gospel during Vespers and Matins. This custom is a historical remnant of the ancient deaconesses who disappeared during the Middle Ages, but survived under some guise within the closed walls of the Carthusian monasteries.

In each female Carthusian monastery one or two monks are responsible for the priestly service within the community, like the celebration of the Eucharist and the administering of the sacrament of penance.

The Monastic Family of Bethlehem

Most people think that the monks and sisters of Bethlehem constitute a branch of the Carthusian order, but in fact they do not. The Monastic Family of Bethlehem, as approved by Rome in 1998, is an autonomous religious institute of pontifical law. The origins of the sisters goes back to 1950, the year in which Pope Pius XII (1939–58) proclaimed the Dogma of the Assumption of the Virgin Mary. Seven French pilgrims were so deeply touched by the message of the Pope that they took the decision to live a life of solitude and prayer in the spirit of St Bruno. This project received concrete form in the little village of Chamvres in Burgundy, where the first monastery was built.[61]

The official name of this new religious institute is 'The Monastic Family of Bethlehem, of the Assumption of the Virgin Mary and of St Bruno'. Such a long name is not without proper significance of course. The original chapel in Chamvres looked like the stall in which Jesus was born, so the monastery received quite spontaneously the name 'Bethlehem'. 'The Assumption of the Virgin Mary' refers to the proclamation of the dogma as the moment of birth and 'St Bruno' to the charisma of solitude and prayer. The monks and the sisters of Bethlehem constitute one monastic family divided into a male and a female branch, both autonomously governed by a prior general and a prioress general.

Like the Carthusians, the monks and the sisters of Bethlehem devote their lives to prayer and labour in their solitary cells. Only morning prayer, the Eucharist and Vespers are celebrated in community. But there are also some remarkable differences between the Carthusian order and the Monastic Family of Bethlehem. First of all the liturgy in Bethlehem is inspired by the Byzantine tradition with a strong cult for icons, while the Carthusians use a Gregorian and Latin repertoire. Furthermore the regime of fasting is less severe and their sleep is not interrupted for midnight prayer in the way of the Carthusians. The most significant difference is in regard to hospitality in Bethlehem: people

---

[61]   The male branch of the Monastic Family of Bethlehem only appeared in 1976.

who desire some days for prayer in solitude and silence are welcome in a special guesthouse or even in a hermit cell. All moments of common prayer are accessible to pilgrims or passers-by. These practices are almost unthinkable in a Carthusian monastery – with some rare exceptions.

The Monastic Family of Bethlehem has no shortage of new vocations and candidates. Today, this new congregation has thirty monasteries for sisters and four for monks, in Italy, Spain, Austria, Germany, Poland, Lithuania, Belgium,[62] Israel, the United States (New York), Canada, Argentina and Chile. Plans are made to expand to Switzerland, Jordan and Mexico.[63] When we asked Dom Marcellin Theeuwes the reason for this success, he answered: 'All new ecclesiastical movements have a lot of candidates. They have something fresh and new and they do not drag ten centuries of history as we do. Maybe that's the reason for their success?'[64]

---

[62] The foundation of a monastery in Belgium was realised in 1999 on the explicit demand of the former King Bauduoin I (1950–93).

[63] For the sixtieth jubilee year in 2010, we published the life story of a sister of Bethlehem we knew very well; cf. T. Peeters, 'De heilige Bruno achterna: getuigenis van een bijzondere roeping', *Het Teken* (83/2010), pp. 139–42.

[64] Snapshot of a personal meeting with the Prior of the Grande Chartreuse on 20 July 2006.

3

The Spiritual Way of Solitude in the Carthusian Order

Silence and solitude: pillars of the Carthusian life

With the following text the Carthusian monks present themselves in the Museum of the Grande Chartreuse: 'They have existed for more than nine hundred years. They walk slowly and alone towards the encounter with God. They take another route than ours. Our route is marked by many daily sorrows. They are dressed in prayer garments. They live celibate lives and they renounce all desires of the flesh and the joy and the pain of family life. Their look avoids the agitation of the world. Although they keep up to date about the most important events in the world, they follow society from a distance and voluntarily restrict themselves on this point. They remain distanced from the violence, the noise and the filthy air of the cities. They live a hidden life. Separated from the world, they entered the solitary desert in order to discover their own limits and poverty. They hope to find peace and communion, joy and fullness of life. And they sing: O blessed solitude!'

Silence and solitude are the pillars of the Carthusian way of life. The small plaque near the main entrance of the Grande Chartreuse leaves pilgrims and tourists in no doubt: 'The monks, who devote their life to God, thank you for respecting the solitude and silence in which they pray and sacrifice for you.' When the Dutch journalist Leo Fijen saw this message near the main gate, he asked Dom Marcellin Theeuwes for some explanation. He answered spontaneously before the camera: 'Our whole life lies in these words: a life of solitude and silence. It is impossible to be a hermit in the midst of noises and sounds. So silence is required. Each solitary monk has his own little house, a hermitage. Indeed, we live alone but at the same time we experience a strong spirit of communion. That is a reality for us every minute of the day. A monk remains for the greater part of his life, alone in his cell. He lives, prays and studies eighteen hours a day in his cell.'[65]

Dom Jacques Dupont, the Prior of Serra San Bruno, who once renounced an academic career at the Sorbonne University in Paris to become a Carthusian monk, illustrates the proper meaning of solitude and silence in monastic life with a beautiful story: 'Yes indeed, we waste our lives because we love Jesus. But anyone who has fallen in love, knows that real love can lead to the biggest follies. A man once asked a hermit: Wise man, speak to me. But the hermit answered: When I speak, my tongue will interrupt silence. So when you ask me to interrupt silence, you will never understand

---

[65]   L. Fijen, *De reis van je hoofd naar je hart*, p. 145.

my message.'[66] Indicating the symbiosis between silence and solitude, Denys the Carthusian wrote the following reflection: 'Silence is both useful and necessary for a monk. That's why our Fathers prescribe that we not only have to avoid trivial, impolite or improper words, but even good, useful and suitable words. They have proscribed that we may never speak without permission, because they were afraid that decent conversations would pour in abundant words and replies ... If you desire monastic perfection and a life of peace in your cell, for your own good: shut and seal your mouth with the excellent cover of silence!'[67]

One of the most exquisite treatises about solitude and silence within the Carthusian tradition is unpretentiously Guigo's *Letter on Solitary Life to an Unknown Friend*. This unique letter, written between 1130 and 1136, was rediscovered after centuries in the archives of the Grande Chartreuse (1933). The letter is directed to an anonymous friend, because the original name was carefully wiped out by a later generation:

> To the Reverend N. From Guigo, least of those servants of the Cross who are in the Charterhouse to live and to die for Christ.
>
> One man will think another happy. I esteem him happy above all who does not strive to be lifted up with great honours in a palace, but who elects, humbly, to live like a poor country man in a hermitage; who

---

66   E. Romeo, *I solitari di Dio. Separati da tutti, uniti a tutti*, p. 75.
67   Denys le Chartreux, *Eloge de la vie en solitude (Spir. Cart.)*, pp. 196, 198.

with thoughtful application loves to meditate in peace; who seeks to sit by himself in silence.

For to shine with honours, to be lifted up with dignitaries is in my judgement a way of little peace. It is subject to perils, burdened with cares, treacherous to many, and secure for none. Living this life is happy in the beginning, perplexing in its development, wretched in its end. It can be flattering to the unworthy, disgraceful to the good, generally deceptive to both and, while it makes many wretched, it satisfies none, and makes no one happy.

But the poor and solitary life, hard in its beginning, easy in its progress, becomes, in its end, heavenly. It is constant in adversity, trusting in hours of doubt, modest in times of good fortune. This life with its sober fare, simple garments, laconic speech, chaste manners, is a higher ambition. Without this ambition, and often wounded with sorrow at the thought of past wrong done, this simple and solitary life avoids present, and is wary of future, evil. Resting on the hope of mercy, without trust in its own merit, it thirsts after heaven, is sick of earth, earnestly strives for right conduct, which it retains in constancy and holds firmly forever. It fasts with determined constancy in love of the cross, yet consents to eat for the body's need. In both it observes the greatest moderation, for when it dines it restrains greed and when it fasts, vanity. It is devoted to reading, but mostly in the Scripture canon and in holy books where it is more intent upon the inner marrow of meaning than on the froth of words. But you may praise or wonder more at this: that such a life is continually idle yet never lazy. For it finds many things indeed to do, so that time is more often lacking to it than this or that occupation. It more often laments that its time has slipped away than that its business is tedious.

What else? A happy subject, to advise leisure, but such an exhortation seeks out a mind that is its own master, concerned with its own business, disdaining to be caught up in the affairs of others, or of society. Whomsoever fights as a soldier of Christ in peace will refuse double service as a soldier of God and a hireling of the world. Who knows for sure it cannot here be glad with this world and then in the next reign with God.

Small matters are these, and their like, if you recall what drink He took at the gibbet, Who calls you to kingship. Like it or not, you must follow the example of Christ who is poor, if you would have fellowship with Christ in His riches. If we suffer with Him, says the Apostle, we shall reign with Him. If we die with Him, then we shall live together with Him. The Mediator Himself replied to the two disciples who asked Him if one of them might sit at His right hand and the other at His left: 'Can you drink the chalice which I am about to drink?' Here He made clear that it is by cups of earthly bitterness that we come to the banquet of the Patriarchs and to the nectar of heavenly celebrations.

Since friendship strengthens confidence I charge, advise and beg you, my best beloved in Christ, dear to me since the day I knew you, that as you are farseeing, careful, learned and most acute, take care to save the little bit of life that remains still unconsumed, snatch it from the world, light under it the fire of love to burn it up as an evening sacrifice to God. Delay not, but be like Christ both priest and victim, in an odour of sweetness to God and to men.

Now, that you may fully understand the drift of all my argument, I appeal to your wise judgement in few words with what is at once the counsel and desire of my soul. Undertake our observance as a man of great heart and noble deeds, for the sake of your eternal salvation. Become a recruit of Christ and stand guard in the camp of the heavenly army, watchful with your sword on your thigh against the terrors of the night.

Here, then, I urge you to an enterprise that is good to undertake, easy to carry out and happy in its consummation. Let prayers be said, I beg you, that in carrying out so worthy a business you may exert yourself in proportion to the grace that will smile on you in God's favour. As to where or when you must do this thing, I leave it to the choice of your own prudence. But to delay or to hesitate will not, as I believe, serve your turn.

I will proceed no further with this, for fear that rough and uncouth lines might offend you, a man of palaces and courts. An end and a measure then to this letter, but never an end to my affection of love for you.[68]

---

[68]   Guigo's Letter on solitary life to an unknown friend (www.chartreux.org).

The desert, a biblical ideal of solitude

The desert: an ambiguous place of abandonment and communion

'Modern culture describes the experience of the desert often as a denial of life, but in fact this is not so. The desert is a silent place, a place where a monk (and indeed any person) can grow in the art of listening. The desert is the place to which people withdraw in order to listen to the voice that speaks to them. Those who are familiar with the Bible know that God says to the prophet Hosea: "I will lead you into the desert and I will speak to your heart" (Hos. 2:14). This text is very sacred to monks because it refers to the ultimate goal of withdrawal to the desert. They leave the world because they want to listen. The desert is a place where communion with God can be deepened and fulfilled. In silence, people will discover their own being in a manner hitherto unimagined. This is only possible through an intentional choice for silence and a desire to reach communion with God. When one chooses the desert for personal gain, one will soon experience it as a trap and will feel locked in terrible isolation.'[69] The proper importance of the desert has been clearly elucidated by an anonymous Carthusian monk:

> What is the significance of the word desert? It is a dry and dangerous place, a harsh and lifeless place where there is immense emptiness. The desert evokes images of sandstorms, burning sun, fat morganas and

---

[69]   I Monaci di Serra San Bruno, *Sentieri del deserto*, p. 63.

scorpions. But the theme of desert is also central to
the Scriptures. In the desert, Moses received his call
and the revelation of the unpronounceable name of
God. In the desert, Elias experienced God's generosity,
patience and mercy. John the Baptist remained in
the desert, preaching to the people of Israel. Jesus
withdrew to the desert to pray, far away from the flock.

From all eternity God calls people into solitude.
There they can find communion with God. Bruno
received such a call. He withdrew with a few
companions into the desert of Chartreuse in the Alps
and later on into the Calabrese Serra. Bruno left us a
testimony to his experience in the desert. He speaks
about paradise, about marriage and about an intimate
communion with God. At the same time he had a
strong experience of struggle and trial. Even Jesus had
to fight the devil in the desert. So one can have intense
experiences in the desert. But these experiences will
contribute to human and spiritual growth, which is so
necessary in our hard and ever-changing world. The
desert always highlights transience and vanity on the
one hand and communion with God on the other. It
is a mistake to see the desert as a refuge, a shelter or
an escape. In the desert, people fight the demons, they
struggle with God and they discover the darkness of
their own being. But ultimately, there is a surrender to
the all-penetrating love of God.

In the experience of Bruno we see another paradox
of the desert. Bruno was never alone because his
solitude was shared by companions who made the same
choice. The Carthusian desert is a desert of fraternal

communion. That is why the monk who withdraws into his cell to enter into his inner self and his heart is able to embrace God and entire humanity with warm and strong love. Solitude carries the monk unto full communion because it bears sweet love. Whoever leaves the world physically will embrace that same world in his heart. Who lives at the edge of society, lives in the heart of the Church and the world![70]

The ambiguity of the desert is clearly expressed in this text: the desert is at the same time a place of abandonment and of communion, of God's presence and God's absence. This is the lifelong struggle of the solitary monk: to seek and to find, to win and to lose, to hope and to despair. In one of his homilies, Dom Jacques Dupont once said:

Those who want to follow Jesus into the desert, will experience that they enter a place of struggle. The Desert Fathers speak about the spiritual struggle as an essential element of monastic life, certainly of the solitary life ... Bruno speaks of an exhausting struggle. Solitude requires courage and strength. Only God's athletes will endure. Guigo even speaks about Carthusian life in military terms: 'Christ's recruits awake in the camp of the divine army with a spirit of holiness and precaution, armed with swords to fight all surprises during the night.' The monastic tradition uses terms which are proper to the letters of St Paul. In line with the Desert Fathers, Bruno understands solitary

---

[70]   Un Certosino, 'Prefazione', in A. Louf, *San Bruno. L'esperienza del deserto*, pp. 5–7.

life as a school, even if he doesn't speak about the classic attempts and temptations which every hermit experiences – greed, apathy, lust, fury, etc. – because he does not want to scare his friend. There is no monastic life without fatigue, anxiety or temptation … The monk has to fight this struggle in his heart, away from the eyes of others. Therefore we have a different kind of struggle from those who hold a visible office in the Church. The Carthusian monk must wrest all weeds from his heart. And we know that these weeds grow very quickly while we are not watching! These poisoned plants are despair, indifference, lust, lamentation, anger, jealousy, etc. The monk has to forego his personal desires. He must be open and willing to surrender to God. When he achieves this he will find true freedom. In this state, the monk is aware of his inner depths in which all fears and masks are removed. The freedom of his heart is not in contradiction with the will of God, because the monk is only free when he dares to live in total dependence on God, from whom he receives everything. This submission is guaranteed by the monastic rule, which is merely a school.[71]

The biblical desert: place of encounter with God

In the Bible, the theme of the desert has always had ambiguous significance: the desert symbolises at the same time the absence of God and the encounter with God. In the seeming lifelessness of the desert, God called his beloved

---

[71]   Un Certosino, *Ferventi di amore divino*, pp. 57, 59–60, 62.

people, God revealed the Ten Commandments and led the flock into the Promised Land. In the desert, Jesus struggled with Satan and felt intimately united with his Father. In the desert, absence and presence, loneliness and communion go hand in hand. This ambiguous significance of the desert in Scripture is the basis of the ancient monastic tradition, which began in the search for solitude and separation by the Desert Fathers. The biblical significance of the desert also inspired Guigo I. In the final chapter of *The Customs of Chartreuse*, entitled 'Praise of Life in Solitude', Guigo I points out the importance of solitude in the lives of great biblical figures like Isaac, Jacob, Moses, Elijah, Elisha, Jeremiah, John the Baptist and ultimately Jesus himself. They all received a divine call or revelation when they were in the desert alone. In the Bible, solitude is a privileged state of grace. 'The book of Deuteronomy explains – more than any other biblical text – the real significance of the affliction of the Jewish People in the desert. "Remember how the Lord your God led you all the way in the wilderness these forty years, to humble and test you in order to know what was in your heart, whether or not you would keep his commands. He humbled you, causing you to hunger and then feeding you with manna, which neither you nor your ancestors had known, to teach you that man does not live on bread alone but on every word that comes from the mouth of the Lord" (Deut. 8:2–3).' In the final chapter of *The Customs of Chartreuse*, Guigo I wrote about the significance of the desert in Scripture:

> For, as you know, in the Old Testament, and still more so in the New, almost all of God's secrets of major

importance and hidden meaning were revealed to His servants, not in the turbulence of the crowd but in the silence of solitude. You know, too, that these same servants of God, when they wished to penetrate more profoundly some spiritual truth, or to pray with greater freedom, or to become a stranger to things earthly in an ardent elevation of the soul, nearly always fled the hindrance of the multitude for the benefits of solitude.

Thus – to illustrate by some examples – when seeking a place for meditation, Isaac went out to a field alone; and this, one may assume, was his normal practice, and not an isolated incident. Likewise, it was when Jacob was alone, having dispatched his retinue ahead of him, that he saw God face to face, and was thus favoured with a blessing and a new and better name, thus receiving more in one moment of solitude than in a whole lifetime of social contact.

Scripture also tells us how Moses, Elijah and Elisha esteemed solitude, and how conducive they found it to an even deeper penetration of the divine secrets; and note, too, what perils constantly surrounded them when among men, and how God visited them when alone.

Overwhelmed by the spectacle of God's indignation, Jeremiah, too, sat alone. He asked that his head might be a fountain, his eyes a spring for tears, to mourn the slain of his people; and that he might the more freely give himself to this holy work he exclaimed: 'O, that I had in the desert a wayfarer's shelter!' (Jer. 9:2), clearly implying that he could not do this in a city, and thus indicating what an impediment companions are to the gift of tears. Jeremiah also said, 'It is good for a man to await the salvation of God in silence' (Lam. 3:26) – which longing solitude greatly favours; and he adds, 'It is good also for the man who has borne the yoke from early youth' (Lam. 3:27) – a very consoling text for us, many of whom have embraced this vocation from early manhood; and yet again he speaks, saying, 'The solitary will sit and keep silence, for he will lift himself above himself' (Lam. 3:28). Here the prophet makes reference to nearly all that is best in our life: peace, solitude, silence, and ardent thirst for the things of heaven. Later, as an example of the supreme patience and perfect humility of those formed in this school, Jeremiah speaks of 'Jeering of the multitude and cheek buffeted in scorn, bravely endured' (Lam. 3:30–32).

John the Baptist, greater than whoever, the Saviour tells us, has not arisen among those born of women, is another striking example of the safety and value of solitude. Trusting not in the fact that divine prophecy had foretold that he would be filled with the Holy Spirit from his mother's womb, and that he would go before Christ the Lord in the 'spirit and power' of Elijah (Luke 1:11–17); nor in the fact that his birth had been miraculous, and that his parents were saints, he fled the society of men as something dangerous and chose the security of desert solitude (Luke 1:80); and, in actual fact, as long as he dwelt alone in the desert, he knew neither danger nor death. Moreover the virtue and merit he attained there are amply attested by his unique call to baptise Christ, and by his acceptance of death for the sake of justice. For, schooled in sanctity in solitude, he alone of all men became worthy to wash Christ (Mtat. 3:13–17) - Christ who washes all things clean – and worthy, too, to undergo prison bonds and death itself in the cause of truth (Matt. 14:3–12).

Jesus himself, God and Lord, whose virtue was above both the assistance of solitude and the hindrance of social contact, wished nevertheless to teach us by his example; so before beginning to preach or work miracles he was, as it were, proved by a period of fasting and temptation in the solitude of the desert; similarly, Scripture speaks of him leaving his disciples and ascending the mountain alone to pray. Then there was that striking example of the value of solitude as a help to prayer when Christ, just as his Passion was approaching, left even his Apostles to pray alone – a clear indication that solitude is to be preferred for prayer even to the company of Apostles ...

And now, dear reader, ponder and reflect on the great spiritual benefits derived from solitude by the holy and venerable Fathers – Paul, Antony, Hilarion, Benedict, and others without number – and you will readily agree that for the spiritual savour of psalmody; for penetrating the message of the written page; for kindling the fire of fervent prayer; for engaging in profound meditation; for losing oneself in mystic contemplation; for obtaining the heavenly dew of purifying tears, nothing is more helpful than solitude.[72]

---

[72]   *Praise of Life in Solitude* (www.chartreux.org).

Completely in line with the final chapter of *The Customs of Chartreuse*, Guigo II, the ninth Prior of the Grande Chartreuse, also wrote a hymn to solitary life in one of his *Twelve Meditations*. The text is written at the end of the twelfth century: 'O sweet Jesus … Unhappy is the solitary who doesn't know You as his single company. So many people live among the crowd and still feel lonely, because they are not with You. Help me to be with You, than I shall never be alone … "He sits in solitude" is what we read in Scripture. When a solitary is content, he never feels alone … Who can't be alone, neither can be silent. And who can't be silent, isn't capable to listen to You.'[73]

John the Baptist: a biblical example of solitude and asceticism

St John the Baptist holds a prominent place in the Carthusian tradition as a biblical example of the solitary life par excellence. This remarkably fine prophet waited for the coming of Christ in the desert, where he filled his days with prayer and sacrifice. It is not by accident that an icon of St John the Baptist and one of the Virgin Mary decorate the apse of the church of the Grande Chartreuse. Both icons were painted by the modern French artist Jean-Marie Pirot-Arcabas (b. 1926), who continues to live in the little village of St-Hugues-de-Chartreuse, just a few miles from the Grande Chartreuse. The picturesque parish church became a permanent exhibition place for his paintings and art.

---

[73]   Guiges II le Chartreux, 'Méditation I', in *Lettre sur la vie contemplative. Douze Méditations* (SC 163), pp. 127–9.

An anonymous Carthusian monk once wrote in one of his conferences for novices:

> All our churches are devoted to John the Baptist and the Virgin Mary. As a community of solitary monks we focus on the Virgin who conceived God's Eternal Word in silent faith. But we also focus on John the Baptist, the rough hermit who stands as a sentry on the threshold of God's Kingdom ... Each single monk empathises with this severe, simple, strong and humble man. His voice carries the fruit of silence, the solitude and the prayer of many years. His voice is truthful, because it is a sounding board of the divine truth. John the Baptist *is* a voice: because of his message, he became small and humble. As a man of God he looked to reality with the eyes of faith. He refused to adopt the mentality of the world. He was not afraid to accuse the kings of evil. He understood the signs of his age as the hour of God. Only John the Baptist was able to recognise the Messiah, 'the One who had to come', in that unknown man from Nazareth ... We can only recognise and receive Christ when we are directed by the Holy Spirit. We know the signs of God's Spirit: love, joy, peace, patience, kindness, faithfulness, gentleness, self-control – all these are the works of light. But we also know the signs of the evil spirit: impurity, greed, idolatry, sorcery, hate, enmity, jealousy, disputes, quarrels, envy, etc. (cf. Gal. 5:17–25) – all these are the works of darkness which are inspired by the spirit of darkness. We must focus with a pure heart. So often I was unable to recognise Christ, I just

passed him, because I was blinded by egotistic desires and greed. Each time when I was expecting something extraordinary and spectacular, like the Jewish people did, Christ was alongside me, hidden in the mystery of the smallest event. Indeed, trivial for those who have a distracted look, but it is divine for those who know how to look with the eyes of a child.[74]

The imitation of Christ in the desert

Of course, Jesus Christ is an outstanding example of a life in solitude. Jesus withdrew quite often in solitude to pray. He remained for 40 days and nights in the desert as a period of affliction and strengthening. The same anonymous Carthusian monk wrote about Christ's retreat in the desert: 'This story, which is written in all Synoptic gospels, is read on the first Sunday of Lent. This story does not refer only to an historic event in the life of Jesus, but it describes very dramatically a deeper dimension of Christ's life. Throughout his life, Jesus had to struggle in obedience to his heavenly Father, until he was crucified. This is the proper significance of this story.'[75]

'The ancient Fathers called the lives of the desert monks *apostolic*, because they lived *like the Apostles*. This means they lived in permanent communion with Jesus,' witnesses another Carthusian monk. 'Jesus asked his Apostles to be in continuous communion with Him. Therefore, the contemplative life is a true and specific charisma within the

---

74   UN Chartreux, *Vivre dans l'intimité du Christ* (2005/1), pp. 47, 49, 62–3.
75   UN Chartreux, *Vivre dans l'intimité du Christ* (2005/1), p. 117.

Church. In the way of all other charismas, it contributes to Christ's mission of redemption of all creation. Only the one who remains faithful to his own charisma bears the fruits the people need.'[76] 'The earthly life of Jesus offers many possibilities of imitation. According to Scripture Jesus spent long hours in solitary prayer. The Carthusian monk desires to continue this solitary prayer in the heart of the Church and the world. The monk is one who follows Christ onto the mountain to pray ... Through the joys and sufferings of a life in solitude, the monk tries to unite each day with Christ.'[77] Also Denys the Carthusian referred in his *Praise on Life in Solitude* to the solitary prayer of Jesus as the essence of the hermit life:

> Solitude had an important place in the life of Jesus. During his earthly life, Jesus was able to perform wonderful signs and wonders, but above all the example of his life remains his most important teaching. That is why He always withdrew in solitude before He performed divine actions. St Mark says: 'Jesus got up and went to a lonely place where He could pray.' And even St Luke says: 'Jesus withdrew to a lonely place to pray.' At the moment of his Passion, Jesus removed himself from the presence of his Apostles and his most beloved disciples so that He could pray three times to his Father. He moved further away where He could pray with the greatest fervour and where He

---

[76]   I Monaci di Serra San Bruno, *Sentieri del deserto*, pp. 63–4.
[77]   A. Louf, *San Bruno*, pp. 33, 35.

could meditate on the mysteries of God's redemption of humankind.

The Lord did not like to stay too long with the crowd. The tumult clearly disturbed his intimate communion with God ... St John says that Jesus used to withdraw with his disciples into the garden, even during the night. He wanted to pray, as He did at the moment of his Passion. There is no doubt that Jesus spent time apart from his disciples so that He could pray without distraction. When the Son of God was accustomed to pray regularly and with great attention, then it is true that a lifelong solitary life is praiseworthy in all its perfection.[78]

Three concentric circles of solitude and silence

The notion of the desert signifies solitude and silence within the Carthusian tradition. So a Carthusian 'desert' may not always exist in sand, heat or drought, but rather in isolation, solitude, silence and poverty. A Carthusian 'desert' can be fresh and green, wet or snowy. The desert element is not defined by the climate, but rather by isolation, distance and by the typical architecture of a Carthusian monastery. In the Carthusian 'desert', solitude and silence are the result of a triple enclosure: the isolation of the desert, of the cloister walls and of each solitary cell. The hermitage 'is part of a topography of solitude and repentance. This topography reflects a centripetal dynamic, a movement inside or at the

---

[78]   Denys le Chartreux, *Eloge de la vie en solitude*, pp. 127–8.

centre. Three places of solitude succeed one another as concentric circles. These circles direct the monk more and more intensely to the essence of monastic life: the search for God. The search for solitude is in fact the longing for God.'[79]

The first concentric circle: the territory of the desert

The outermost circle, which has to guarantee solitude and silence, is formed by the geographical position of the monastery, the proverbial desert or *eremus* in Latin. Carthusian monasteries are always – or mostly – located far from the bustle of civilisation. The experience of the past has taught that cities or municipal areas are not suitable locations to realise the Carthusian lifestyle. For this reason all Carthusian monasteries disappeared from the cities for many centuries. The most appropriate location for a life of prayer and contemplation is a hidden and quiet place. 'On this spot, far away from the stir and noise of others, one can devote and entrust one's heart to God with veneration and trust,'[80] so says Denys the Carthusian. 'Solitary life always results in a separation from humanity, from its sight as well as from its activities. The further one is separated from the world … the more one will be able to unite with God in a free, quiet, perfect and durable contemplation, in fervent love, in continuous praise and in spiritual exercises.'[81]

---

[79]   P. Nissen, *Eenzaamheid als zoeken naar God*, p. 100.

[80]   Denys the Carthusian, 'De contemplatione', in *Opera minora*, vol. 41.163 B.

[81]   Denys le Chartreux, *Eloge de la vie en solitude*, p. 149.

The physical or geographical separation from the world, which is so characteristic of strict contemplative life, has been recognised by the authority of the Church and determined in canon law and juridical provisions. The Church desires to protect the original charisma of the monastic orders, of their founders and reformers. The Instruction *Verbi Sponsa*, promulgated by the Roman Congregation for Institutes of Consecrated Life and Societies of Apostolic Life (May 1999), points out that the Catholic tradition always connected strict contemplative life with the solitary prayer of Jesus on the mountain top: 'From the beginning and in a unique way, monasteries devoted to the contemplative life have found the enclosure a proven help in the fulfilment of their vocation. The particular demands of separation from the world have thus been received by the Church and canonically ordered for the benefit of the contemplative life itself. The discipline of enclosure is therefore a gift, for it protects the foundational charisma of monasteries. Every contemplative Institute must faithfully maintain its form of separation from the world … Real separation from the world, silence and solitude, express and protect the integrity and identity of the wholly contemplative life, ensuring that it remains faithful to its specific charisma and to the sound traditions of the Institute. The Church's Magisterium has often restated the need for this manner of life, which is a source of grace and holiness for the Church, to be faithfully maintained.'[82]

---

[82]   *Verbi Sponsa. Instruction on the Contemplative Life and on the Enclosure of Nuns*, 9–10.

An image often used for the separation of the world or the monastic desert is that of the harbour:

> The solitary monk, who left the world, has already reached the harbour. He has escaped from the swirling floods of the world with so many dangers and shipwrecks and has arrived in the 'quiet and safe harbour', as Bruno calls it. Of course we must interpret this expression according to the (technical) significance of the ancient monastic vocabulary. In the monastic tradition, the harbour is represented as *tutus et quietus* [safe and quiet]. The word *quies* or quiet defines one of the most significant qualities of Carthusian life. This quiet or silence refers to the typical location of the Carthusian desert. When Bruno uses the word quiet, he doesn't think about the severe Alps in the Dauphiné, but rather about the sweet harmony of meadows and hills in Calabria. Bruno likes to describe the environment. The quiet of the environment contributes to the inner quiet, the place where God is revealed and Christ is met. The inner quiet of the solitary monk was described in a lively way by Guigo I in this accurate and simple expression: a Carthusian must be a *quietus Christo*: his inner quiet must be devoted entirely to Christ.[83]

The image of the harbour is also used in the letters of the first Carthusian monks of Portes: 'Try to reach the safety of the harbour. A navigator who stops at a bank during a

---

[83]   A. Louf, *San Bruno*, pp. 18–19.

storm while he could reach the safe harbour quite easily, will rightly be accused of incompetence. Why should you steer the ship on the high seas when you fear already a shipwreck at the bank? Why should you escape from the storm when a small sandbank is already capable of breaking the stern of the ship? Consider seriously! Be a vigilant and faithful navigator for your soul. Never be cowardly – if you ever were – because this kind of weakness will not please God.'[84]

In a conference to a Belgian Trappist community, Cardinal Danneels once used a similar metaphor to speak about the quiet or *quies* of contemplative life. He compared the monks with the 'eye in the hurricane':

> Last week, I read a beautiful comparison about the identity of the contemplative orders and contemplative men in human history. When you see an aerial photograph of a hurricane, you see a string of clouds. But in the centre you see the so-called eye of the hurricane. It is quiet, immovable and without wind. In the middle of the storm, a small slice of silence is saved: total quiet. It is the eye of the hurricane. More than ever, the world in which we live is like a hurricane. A hurricane of nervous searching and wandering, a chaos often of impasse and of oscillation. Everything moves. But in the middle of this hurricane, God saved the eye of a still point of perfect quiet: who enters will find quiet, calm, order and serenity.

---

[84] Jean De Portes, 'Lettre à son frère Etienne', in *Lettres des premiers Chartreux* (SC 274), p. 143.

It is impossible to avoid the turbulences of our time – even turbulence produces good things. Our world suffers in the pain of new birth. Happy are those who know that there is an eye of quiet in the middle of the storm – especially those who reach it. They can live in the centre of the storm, as the eye is in the centre. They have found quiet, stability and balance. The contemplative man lives in such a place, a site of peace, calm and serenity. He *is* that eye … It is my pastoral experience – long before I became a bishop – that you can only make people happy when you offer them quiet, serenity and peace. Not by means of many words and reason, but by means of an atmosphere of peace. Most people who have problems do not ask for solutions, but simply for peace. They want to meet a person who emanates real peace. Someone who understands their problems and who cares for them, but who is in the first place totally concentrated on God, someone with a sense for God … If there are no people who risk their lives for the Gospel, the faithful may lose all orientation. Without radical exemplars, ordinary Christians may lose their spirit. This is your mission! Without exemplars of total surrender, God will disappear in our secular world. We believe in a self-giving God, who came into our world and who revealed his being in his Son Jesus Christ. So you have to go to the limit, of course according to your abilities. Be poor, pure and obedient and try to attain the limit![85]

In the Carthusian tradition, the desert is also understood as an inner reality, maybe even stronger than as an external one. Solitude and silence must be inside a person: in the heart or the inner being of the monk. The external framework of the desert will help the solitary monk in descending into the depths of his inner self and to meet God. 'The solitary will sit and keep silence, for he will lift himself above himself.' With this paraphrase from the book of Lamentations, Guigo I wants to point out that 'this descent in your inner self or in your own being is at the same time a movement of ascending or elevating yourself ... At this point, the Carthusian monk participates in the dynamic of God's love. This is what Bruno desires for his friend Ralph: to be inflamed by this divine love: "I should like for you, too, dear brother, to love God above all, so that warmed by his embrace you may be aflame with divine love." In this fiery encounter of love, the dynamic topography of solitude will reach its goal. On this point, the blessed solitude becomes the only beatitude.'[86] After many years of perseverance and patience, Carthusian monks 'do not feel lonely or locked in their cells, they simply live in solitude and silence. On the contrary, the release from the material world provides them with happiness and freedom.'[87]

---

[85] G. Danneels, 'Het oog in de orkaan', in Abdij van Westmalle, *Stilte aan het woord*, pp. 12–13, 20.

[86] P. Nissen, *Eenzaamheid als zoeken naar God*, p. 103.

[87] M. D Roeck, *Kardinaal Danneels over Into Great Silence*, p. 1.

In the past, the separation from the world was often called 'dying to the world'. Denys the Carthusian uses this expression regularly. But when the word 'dying' is understood all too literally, all sorts of Spartan fantasies and even macabre myths will appear about monastic life. Some of these myths allege that Carthusians have to dig their own grave or greet each other by saying: *Memento mori* (Remember you will die). In Italy, a legend appeared about the Carthusian monastery in Serra San Bruno: one of the monks would be the American soldier who dropped the atomic bomb on Hiroshima. He became a hermit to repent for his sin. In 1962, this legend was published in several newspapers and even reported on the national television. 'No one becomes a Carthusian monk to die, but to live!', once wrote a Carthusian monk from La Valsainte in Switzerland. 'The dying to the world and to your own will is only a means. Life is the ultimate goal, a life of communion with God. "I came to give them life, and truly in abundance" (John 10:10) … This positive aspect of our lives is often forgotten, because the negative aspect of sacrifice is often exaggerated. Those who become Carthusian monks give their lives for Jesus and share in his sacrifice. Incorporated in Christ, we are incorporated in his death and in his grave, but also in his resurrection and eternal life.'[88] Denys the Carthusian wrote the following thoughts about dying to the world:

> May the cell in which you live let you understand that you are dead and buried for the world. You only

---

[88]   Un Chartreux, *Ecoles de Silence*, pp. 93–4.

have to be alive for Christ. Make no mistake, this is quite appropriate for our form of religious life: not to seek any consolation, comfort or benefit during our earthly life, to refuse all homages, to rejoice in being submissive and despised, to desire poverty, to drive out all temptations and desires. We do not withdraw to a cell to enjoy quiet, power or pleasure, but to sacrifice and to challenge. That is the reason why we withdraw to the desert: to die for God each day ...

It is useless to leave the world physically if we keep it in our heart through evil and carnal desires. You do not dismiss God's creatures because they are creatures or because they might be evil, rather because they may be obstacles in the way which leads to God. If our desires concentrate on creatures, what is the benefit of being separated from them physically and for such lengths of time?[89]

We would like to give an impression out of the famous booklet *The White Paradise* from Pieter Van de Meer de Walcheren (1880–1970), written around Christmas 1926 during his stay in the Carthusian monastery of La Valsainte in Switzerland. We have to admit that the spirituality and language of the Dutch poet may sound a little bit old-fashioned. However, the separation of the world is described by him in a sublime way:

There is no sun yet. It is hidden behind the mountain which closes the highest valley in the east. When

---

[89]   Denys le Chatreux, *La vie et la fin du solitaire* (Spir. Cart.), pp. 5–56.

we walk through the garden at the backside of the Carthusian hermitages, into the deep, dry snow, the glow on the sharp summit of the mountains becomes stronger and stronger. It is perfectly still in this white world. Everything is white. The roofs are white and the mountains are white because of a flat, soft and immaculate blanket of snow. Only here and there some black spots of forests on the inclines, and above them naked rocks rise high. The day becomes white and gold, because suddenly sunlight falls out of the cold into the valley, over the white mountain ridge. The day flourishes. The world is touched by light, as a soul by grace. I watch and listen. Only silence, very deep silence is alive, it breathes all around me and even in me, it penetrates to the depth of my heart as an inexpressible presence.

In the north, the valley is closed by the wide amphitheatre of a mountain. The white mountain linings around me at my left and right. Before me, at the southwest in the valley of the Javroz, streams cut deeply into a small watercourse under a skin of ice. Above the silent buildings of the monastery and the Carthusian dwellings, blue smoke flutters here and there out of a chimney. This monastery is like a glittering crystal, so purely faceted, which has fallen right out from heaven. It lays down in an almost insupportable, breath-taking silence. Now that I know the position and the external face of the monastery, it is time to enter into its living heart.[90]

The second concentric circle: the walled monastery complex

The second concentric circle that protects the solitude and silence is the typical architecture of the Carthusian monastery. High and impenetrable walls separate it from the outside world. The monastery complex guarantees an infrastructure of isolation and quiet. 'The proper architecture of a Carthusian monastery helps each monk to feel at ease in his cell. Guigo's *Consuetudines Cartusiae* contain many concrete measures to guarantee and protect as much as possible the personal solitude of each monk, for example particular measures about liturgy.'[91] One of these measures concerns the daily celebration of the Eucharist, which has only been practised in the Carthusian order since 1222. Other measures maximising solitude and separation within the cloister walls are the restriction of guests and beggars and the abolition of processions. In *The Customs of Chartreuse* we read the following:

> Mass is seldom sung here, because silence and solitude in the cells are our principal intention and concern ... It is important to notice that we never keep processions for whatever solemnity and that feasts or vigils are never transferred. Only religious are allowed as guests during choir. It is allowed to have a common meeting with them in the cloister. Without permission from the

---

90   P. Van der Meer de Walcheren, *Het witte paradijs*, pp. 49–50.
91   P. Nissen, *Eenzaamheid als zoeken naar God*, p. 101.

prior it is forbidden to take someone apart or to be taken apart by someone, either to blabber secrecies to them or to ask them certain favours for others. Besides, the guests themselves – and not us – have to ask this permission if they think it is of great concern ...

We only take care of the guests and not of their mounts. We give them the same beds and the same meals as we use ourselves. Their horses may of course not lack the basic necessities ... May our guests understand how poor, hard and infertile the desert is in which we live, and that we possess nothing outside the desert, no properties and no incomes. The number of guests must be limited, because we only have a few meadows and even fewer fruits from the harvest. We do not have enough food for our own animals, so that is why they have to hibernate outside the desert. And we add that we abhor absolutely the custom of wandering and begging ...

We give bread or other alms to the poor depending on what our goods make possible. It is really exceptional to receive them into our house. We would rather send them to the village to spend the night. We did not withdraw to this solitary desert to care for the material welfare of the stranger, but to gain eternal salvation of our souls. Therefore it is not possible that we should have more attention for those who come to us because of spiritual needs than for those who come for material needs. Otherwise we would not withdraw to such a rugged, isolated and almost inaccessible place.[92]

Even today Carthusian monks retain the fundamental principle to limit the number of guests as much as possible. Parents and close relatives may visit their son or daughter, brother or sister, uncle or aunt, once or twice a year. The visit of friends is rather exceptional. One of the young monks of the Charterhouse in Serra San Bruno witnesses to the reality of separation from his family and friends: 'At the beginning, the separation was very hard. But his parents accepted his choice, because they saw their son was happy in the monastery. "My parents tell me: many parents feel unhappy when their children leave for studies or a job. We know that you are happy here. You are far away from us, but happy. And we know that you pray for us." I made a very radical choice and I had to overcome many obstacles and even good things. But life is a continuing journey of death and resurrection. No choice is free from anguish. The choice to become a Carthusian monk is very noble, which does not mean that other choices are not. A Carthusian monastery is a place where life is concentrated on unity. Each religious vocation – and certainly a Carthusian vocation – is a story of leaving behind'[93] – but it is so much more an embrace of freedom to love God and others with enthusiasm.

The Carthusian order is held to papal enclosure, which means that the entrance of women in male monasteries or

92   *Customs of Chartreuse*, 6, 1; 10, 2; 14, 5; 19, 1–2; 20, 1.
93   E. Romeo, *I solitari di Dio*, pp. 7–8.

men in female monasteries is strictly prohibited. Although, there are some exceptions. In 2001, the Belgian Queen Paolo, who was born in Calabria, visited the Carthusian monks in Serra San Bruno and joined the community for Vespers. And Nathalie Nabert, the former Dean of the Faculty of Arts at the Catholic Institute in Paris and the founder of the Centre de Recherches et d'Etudes de Spiritualité Cartusienne (CRESC)[94], regularly meets various Carthusian monks for her scientific research. Regarding the prohibition for women or men to enter male or female Carthusian monasteries she says: 'If you make a choice to separate from the world and to devote your life entirely to God, you need to give up most connections. It is quite logical that Carthusian monks do not accept women into the monastery or Carthusian nuns do not accept men. The Virgin Mary is the mother of all contemplatives: she shows the monks the right way towards silence, obedience, prayer, charity and patience. However, while the Carthusian monks live separate from all women, it is a woman who watches over them.'[95]

Of course, there is a direct link between celibacy and the prohibition for men or women to enter male or female Carthusian monasteries. 'It is necessary to ... break all boisterous impulses of the flesh and to purify the spirit from all vain and impure thoughts and all evil desires. We must expel everything that stimulates human sensuality.'[96] These words of Denys the Carthusian leave no doubt. In

---

[94] Centre for Research and Study of Carthusian Spirituality, Catholic Institute, Paris.
[95] E. Romeo, *I solitari di Dio*, pp. 51–2.
[96] Denys le Chartreux, *Eloge de la vie en solitude*, p. 145.

The Customs of Chartreuse, Guigo I was also aware of the enormous problems which can arise in a monk's direct contact with women, teenagers or children: they can stimulate sexual desires and disturb the inner peace of the monks. That is why he raised the minimum age of new candidates to 20 years. Guigo's concern even sounds striking today, when we think about all the cases of sexual abuse and paedophilia that have scandalised the Catholic community in so many countries recently.[97] 'The woman as a vamp, as a risk for celibacy? Or the woman as a consolation, has seen the pious devotion for the Virgin Mary of the Carthusian monks? … The physical and visible separation of the other sex may seem an anachronism or an unnatural measure. But in fact it is a very wise measure, because it is founded on the search for a deeper communion with God and therefore with others.'[98] Guigo's description of women has to be understood within the historical context and the theological concepts of the Middle Ages. But above all, his only concern was to avoid problems, excesses and scandals:

> We absolutely don't admit women into the limits of the desert, because we all know that neither the wise

---

[97]   Cf. T. Peeters (annotation note 164), in Guigo De Kartuizer, *Gewoonten. Een leefregel voor kluizenaars in gemeenschap*, p. 90: 'In the history of religious life there are many examples of children who were sent to a monastery for an education. Many rules and constitutions contain prescriptions about this subject, just as the *Rule of St Benedict* does. The Carthusian order dissociates from this tradition. Guigo did not only think about certain sexual excesses, but he was also concerned about the demise of silence, solitude and other monastic observations because of the presence of children in the monastery. Other motivations to refuse children and teenagers were the cold climate and the proper demands of solitary life.'

[98]   E. Romeo, *I solitari di Dio*, pp. 51–2.

man, nor the prophet, nor the judge, nor the guest of
God, nor the sons of God, not even the first man who
was created by God's hands, was able to escape from
the caresses and artifices of women. We think about
Solomon, David, Samson, Lot, all men who took
women who pleased them, and also about Adam. For
a man it is impossible to control the flame in his belly,
or to walk over hot coals without burning his feet, or
to touch the pitch without sticking to it ...

We don't receive children or young adolescents,
because we see with tears how many terrible problems
they cause in certain monasteries. We fear all spiritual
and physical dangers. So we only receive men who have
at least accomplished the age of twenty, young men
who are able to battle the sacred struggle according to
the prescription of Moses.[99]

The fundamental principle of strict separation from
the world implies that the Carthusian order renounces
each pastoral service, predication or administration of
sacraments. Therefore, they don't administer parishes, they
don't preach in public churches and they don't receive guests
for retreats or even for Mass, office prayer, confession or
spiritual conversations – except on rare occasions. Each
Carthusian monastery has a modest guesthouse for relatives,
friends or potential candidates. Some monasteries even have

[99]   *Customs of Chartreuse*, 21, 1–2; 27, 1.

an outside chapel where pilgrims can pray and where Mass is celebrated on Sunday or during summer.[100]

Certainly it is this issue that invites criticism about the ultimate sense of the Carthusian lifestyle from convinced Catholics. What is the Carthusian monk's contribution to the life of the Church, when they do not engage in pastoral or sacramental care? What is the sense of such a (literally) hidden life? The monks are completely separated from modern society, enclosed in a walled fortress or in a high ivory tower of solitude and silence. Is this kind of lifestyle a justified imitation of Christ? These are just a few of the questions people have when they think about the contemplative life. Some visitors in the Museum of the Grande Chartreuse, or at Serra San Bruno, instantly show their scepticism or even their disapproval or judgement! The Carthusian monks seem strange, useless and above all anachronistic. Others, who do not merely think in terms of immediate utility or efficiency, show their respect, their admiration and even sympathy for these solitary seekers of God. 'A strict contemplative and spiritual life cannot be described in terms of utility,' says Cardinal Danneels when he was asked about the film *Into Great Silence*. 'The Carthusian order holds a significant question mark for modern humanity. Many wonder *why* it exists and search for answers. Maybe this is the most significant aspect of the

---

[100]   Even the Great Charterhouse has an outside chapel where a monk celebrates Mass for pilgrims and tourists at 8 a.m.

film: it shows the Carthusian order as a big question mark – it is a documentary without answers!'[101]

Perhaps the Carthusian order appears anachronistic nowadays; however, they have continued to exist for more than nine centuries. 'The world has radically changed during the last decades,' alleges Dom Marcellin Theeuwes. 'Modern society seems to have lost its taste for the invisible and the transcendent level of existence. There is a plurality of convictions, opinions and spiritual messages. Religious practice shrinks everywhere and is often coloured by doubts and fanaticism. The tremendous need for immediacy and efficiency leaves almost no space for tasting spiritual and transcendent realities. A radical choice for God is for most people quite difficult to understand. Monastic life becomes a marginal phenomenon, even for many faithful Catholics. However, in this uncertain society there are men and women who understand the relativity of existence and recognise the authenticity and beauty of the divine in a transcendent reality. Certainly they are less than in the past, but their experience is no less strong. Their vocation affects their total personality and forces them to direct their lives towards one single purpose – unity with God.'[102]

And Dom Marcellin also tells this beautiful story:

---

[101]　M. De Roeck, *Kardinaal Danneels over Into Great Silence*, p. 3. Cf. about the position of the Carthusian order in the communion of the Church: T. Peeters, 'Vivere nel cuore della Chiesa. I certosini e la communio ecclesiale', *Claretianum. Commentaria Theologica Opera et Studio Instituti Theologiae Vitae Consecratae* XLIX, Rome, 2009, pp. 195–206.

[102]　M. Theeuwes, Préface, in Musée Dauphinois (ed.), *La Grande Chartreuse. Au-delà du silence*, p. 6.

When I was a novice in Sélignac, I met an older, but very exceptional friar. When he was young, he wanted to become a forester in Nancy [Northern France]. During our weekly walks, he often stopped when he saw a beautiful flower or a tree. During such a walk, he told me one day: 'I am an old man, but my whole life I have tried to live my vocation faithfully. But there is one thing that troubles me without having an answer: what have I done for others?' ... It is one of the questions people have. But we do not need to blame ourselves. Even the most generous philanthropist is limited in his action. He can only reach a small section of humanity. He cannot embrace all the suffering in this world, neither can he reveal his love for the entire planet. He must learn to be content with helping that which is within his reach. Only Christ's love is universal and effective and that is our main concern as hermits, as a community of solitary monks. We share a spirit of fraternity, which can be difficult on a daily basis. Our community is a miniature world, a microcosm, which appears to be a real grace for each other. With an open heart we try to include everyone.[103]

With a wholesome dose of humour, Dom Jacques Dupont calls his life even foolish: 'Indeed, we waste our lives for Jesus because we love him. But whoever has fallen in love, knows that love is capable of the greatest foolishness!'[104]

---

[103] S. Pruvot, *Entretien avec Dom Marcellin*, pp. 13–14.
[104] E. Romeo, *I solitari di Dio*, pp. 82–3.

The conclusion of Denys' tractate on the purpose of solitary life focuses on this matter. The title of his tractate is sublime: 'Is the solitary monk good-for-nothing and is he really alone?':

> The question begs itself: is a solitary monk really alone or is he a good-for-nothing, is it only a matter of words and not of good sense? Among the Fathers of the Church, their opinion does not differ. Some think that a solitary monk is never alone because God is with him; neither is he a good-for-nothing because a contemplative life is very active. This is the opinion of St Bernard and many others. But others believe that a hermit or an anchorite is indeed *alone* and is *good-for-nothing*. St Augustine describes the life of Mary [Martha's sister] – who chose the better part – as a way of doing nothing! … It is quite understandable that some authors come to this conclusion, because they are using a very specific word. The word *alone* may suggest sadness, as in the writings of St Bernard. In this case, the definition does not express the fullness of the concept. If the word *alone* means to live without an immediate partner, of course the solitary is even more alone than others; because he lives in a supernatural and strangely hidden way. It is correct to call someone a good-for-nothing when he does not do anything useful, but lives only for pleasure and fun. But someone who keeps a certain distance from all external activities and places a focus on inner and divine realities is even called a good-for-nothing. If I am not mistaken, it is

quite clear that solitary life has to be understood in the second manner and not in the first.[105]

Pope John Paul II states that the separation from the world, which is realised by monastic enclosure, is a specific way of the imitation of Christ. In his letter *Vita Consecrata*, published in 1994 after the synod on religious life, he says that by choosing an enclosed space monks and cloistered nuns 'share in Christ's emptying of himself by means of a radical poverty, expressed in their renunciation not only of things but also of "space", of contacts, of so many benefits of creation ... The cloister brings to mind that *space in the heart* where every person is called to union with the Lord. Accepted as a gift and chosen as a free response of love, the cloister is the place of spiritual communion with God and with the brethren, where the limitation of space and contacts works to the advantage of interiorising Gospel values.'[106]

Also the *Roman Instruction on Contemplative Enclosure* stipulates that 'the cloistered desert helps greatly in the pursuit of purity of heart understood in this way, because it reduces to the bare minimum the opportunities for contact with the outside world, lest it disrupt the monastery in different ways, disturbing its atmosphere of peace and holy union with the one Lord ... In this way the cloister eliminates in large part the dispersion which comes from many unnecessary contacts; from the accumulation of

---

[105]   Denys le Chatreux, *La vie et la fin du solitaire*, pp. 8–83.
[106]   *Vita Consecrata*, 59.

images, which are often a source of worldly thoughts and vain desires; of news and emotions which distract from the one thing necessary and dissipate interior harmony. 'In the monastery everything is directed to the search for the face of God, everything is reduced to the essential, because the only thing that matters is what leads to him … In consequence, the regulation of the cloister, in its practical aspects, must be such that it allows the realisation of this sublime contemplative ideal, which implies total dedication, undivided attention, emotional wholeness and consistency of life.'[107]

In a previous chapter we noted that the typical architecture of a Carthusian monastery goes back to the time of St Bruno. High in the Chartreuse massif, the first Carthusians built a stone church and some wooden hermitages, connected by a covered gallery. Throughout the ages, this architectural plan was preserved in its originality for the most part. Subsequently many general chapters of the Carthusians insisted on uniformity among the different monasteries around the world. A notable change, however, was the abolition of the so-called *inferior house* for the friars. Nowadays, they have their own cells or rooms in the *small cloister*, so they live under the same roof as the monks.

A Carthusian monastery consists of three parts, which constitute a perfect harmony between solitude, community life and material maintenance. The most typical part of a monastery complex is the rectangular or square *great cloister*, which connects the monks' hermitages. Small monasteries

---

[107]   *Verbi Sponsa*, 4.

such as Portes or Serra San Bruno only have 12 or 13 hermitages, while huge monasteries like La Valsainte or Parkminster in Southern England (Sussex) have many more, sometimes double, or even 35, similar to the Grande Chartreuse. The cemetery mostly lies in the middle of the great cloister.

The size of some of these cloisters is quite astonishing. With its 0.13 miles at both sides and its 113 windows, the cloister of the Grande Chartreuse is the largest in Europe. Another amazing structure is the baroque and artistic cloister of the former Carthusian monastery of San Lorenzo in Padula (Southern Italy). But, in the centre of all these large or small cloisters, perfect silence reigns. Those who have had the opportunity to visit a Carthusian monastery will have experienced the sense of entering the living heart of a completely separated world: behind the doors in the cloisters, solitary monks live, pray and work for their entire lives. Each door is marked with a letter from the alphabet, according to the ancient tradition of the Desert Fathers. Beside each door is a service-hatch with two little doors: one at the inside of the cell and one at the outside of the cloister. In this service-hatch, the friars place the daily meals of the monks without interrupting their solitude and silence. The monks from their side can leave messages requesting their needs and desires, for example to ask for bread or butter.

The architecture of the monastery guarantees solitude and silence in the monks' cells. Fraternal communion is an essential element of Carthusian life. This was always the case! In the *Biography of St Hugh of Lincoln,*[108] written in the beginning of the thirteenth century, we read a few impressions about a visit to the Grande Chartreuse in 1165. One of Hugh's impressions concerns the mutual fraternity among the solitary monks: 'Their rule prescribes solitude, but not isolation. They live in separate cells, but they are of one heart. Each monk lives on his own, but not for his own sake and the monks own no personal possessions. They combine solitude and community life. They live in solitude because they do not wish to disturb one another; but they also live in community so that no one is deprived of fraternal assistance.'[109]

Even centuries later, the atmosphere is still the same, so witnesses a Carthusian monk: 'Our cells are real hermitages, but they are not spread out in the forest or in the field. The cell of one monk adjoins that of another. Our cells are connected by the cloister, which brings us to the church, chapter and refectory. These are places of fraternal encounter. We have a vocation for solitary life, so we are happy when we are alone in our cells. That's the reason why we live in separate houses. However, we share a great part of community life, especially on Sundays … The Carthusian rhythm does not consist in alternate moments in common and moments of solitude. The Carthusian monk lives in community, even when he is alone in his cell. And he feels the solitude, even when he

---

[108]   St Hugh of Lincoln (d. 1200), or Hugh of Avalon, entered the Grande Chartreuse as a noble Frenchman. In 1179 he was appointed Prior of the Witham Charterhouse in Somerset, the first Carthusian monastery in England. In 1186 he was consecrated Bishop of Lincoln.

[109]   D. L. Douie, H. Farmer (eds), *The Life of St Hugh of Lincoln*, vol. I, p. 23.

The monastery of Grande Chartreuse, near Grenoble, the mother house of the Carthusian order.

Main entrance of Grande Chartreuse.

All photographs copyright © Grande Chartreuse.

Carthusian monk at prayer in his cell.

A monk in the garden of his cell.

A Carthusian brother distributing meals to the cells of hermit monks.

A Carthusian monk eats a meal alone in his cell.

Praying together in the church.

*Celebrating
Holy Mass in
solitude.*

The Chartreuse near Grenoble.

Weekly walks in the snow.

Common prayer time in church.

Sunday recreation.

Interior of the Church of the Grande Chartreuse.

The cemetery of the Grande Chartreuse.

is among his brothers.'[110] Dom Johan De Bruijn, a Dutch
monk who lives in the Charterhouse of Transfiguration in
Arlington (Vermont, USA), confirms this spirit of fraternity
by saying that 'only an *authentic solitude for God* is able to
provide access to the life of God. God acts by means of a
mutual self-giving love from Person to person. That is why
attention for fellow brothers is an essential part of solitary
life ... The love of God which is experienced in the solitary
cell will spill unto the fellow brothers, and as a result a warm
climate of fraternal kindness will deepen quiet and silence
in the solitary cell. Every monastic community is a *school of
love* in which brothers lead one another and become signs
of God's love for each other. Within the community, each
member is inspiring another ... While Carthusian monks
live in solitude, there is a real mutual influence, strengthened
by regular moments of encounter.'[111]

The second great part of a Carthusian monastery consists
of the communal buildings, the church, chapter, refectory,
library, etc. Certain workplaces are housed in this part of
the monastery complex: for example, the kitchen or the
laundry. Very often there are reception rooms for the guests
and the family of the prior, the procurator (economist) and
other monks. Only in moments allowed by the statutes may
the monks leave their cells to join one of these communal
spaces. A visit to the library is always allowed.

---

[110]   Un Certosino, *Ferventi d' amore divino* ..., pp. 28—9.
[111]   J. De Bruijn, 'De Gulden Brief nog leesbaar?', *Benedictijns Tijdschrift* (2001/3), pp.
128–9.

In the final large section of the monastery there are workplaces for the friars: joinery, a forge, a bakery, stores, barns, a farm, a vegetable garden, orchards, and so on. All these workplaces are built a certain distance from the great cloister to safeguard silence and good order. Faithful to the fundamental principle of separation from the world, a Carthusian monastery is self-financing and self-sufficient as far as possible.

In the Grande Chartreuse the ancient *plant room* is still in use. The spices to produce the world-famous Carthusian elixir Chartreuse are dried and kept there. The secret recipe dates from the year 1605. It contains at least 130 different spices which constitute the basis of the green liqueur of 55 degrees and the sweet yellow liqueur of 40 degrees. Throughout history, different personalities tried to steal or to decode the secret composition of spices. But even today, the Carthusian order refuses to reveal this mysterious secret. Since 1935, the alcoholic drinks are produced in Voiron, a village about 15 miles from the Grande Chartreuse. The composition of the spices is still held by the monks. Each year, more than 150,000 tourists visit the distillery in Voiron to taste and buy a variety of goods produced by the Carthusians. The assortment is extensive, consisting of wines, fruity liqueurs, tea and biscuits. The profit is enough to provide for the sustenance of the entire Carthusian order, both male and female branches. It is obvious that the secret recipe of the elixir captures the imagination of many people and heightens many of the mysteries surrounding Carthusian life.

The third concentric circle: the cell of the solitary monk

The last concentric circle that protects the solitude and silence of the monastery is the cell of each single monk. The Carthusian monk's cell may be compared to the middle annual ring of a triennial tree, which is surrounded by two larger annual rings: the territory of the desert and the walled monastery complex. These are the three concentric circles of the topography of solitude and repentance. The third movement of the centripetal dynamic of monastic life ends in the solitary cell. The cell moves the monk towards the true centre of his life: his own heart, his inner self, his soul where God is present. So it is not the cell but the heart of the monk which is the true centre of this dynamic movement! The solitude of the cell is only a means – not a goal – to reach the nucleus of monastic life: the contemplation of God. The monk's heart is compared to a compass point, from which every movement starts and towards which every movement leads. 'Only from God and only for God, that's the essence of solitude,'[112] wrote Pieter Van de Meer de Walcheren in his booklet *The White Paradise*. The Carthusian writings often speak of the difference and, at the same time, the connection between the *external cell* and the *inner cell*, that is, the heart of the monk. William of St Thierry referred to allegory in his *Golden Epistle*: 'The external cell and the inner cell are not the same thing. The external cell is the place in which your soul and your body live. The inner cell is your conscience, in which your soul lives in communion

---

[112]   P. Van de Meer de Walcheren, *Het witte Paradijs*, p. 78.

with God, as the most Beloved among all beloved ones. The gate from the external monastery is a symbol for the gate of an inner rampart: the first gate prohibits the corporal senses to dwell outside, the second gate of the senses of the soul leads to the most intimate place where thought and emotion reside.'[113]

The Latin word *cella* (cell) is derived from the Greek *kellia* or *kellion*, which in ancient monasticism referred to the cabin or the cave to which a hermit withdrew. In the *Rule of St Benedict* the word *cella*, however, is used for the dormitory (communal bedroom), the hospital and even the guesthouse in a monastery. So the original significance of the word *cella* changed throughout time: 'instead of the dwelling of a solitary monk, it became the word used for all kinds of communal spaces in a monastery ... In the writings of the early Carthusian tradition, the word *cella* reclaimed its original significance. The *cella* is the space where a hermit is physically alone. In the *Consuetudines Cartusiae* ... the *cella* is the most important place of dwelling for a Carthusian monk. In most of the eighty chapters of the *Consuetudines* the cell is mentioned, sometimes in the margin, sometimes quite explicitly as the place where the Carthusian must search for and hold solitude ... So the Carthusian became once again a solitary desert monk.'[114] Even the actual statutes of the Carthusian order point out the *cella* as the principal place where the monk remains alone for the greater part of his life. The *cella* is called the *holy ground* where God and man

[113] William of St Thierry, *Golden Epistle*, pp. 227–9.
[114] P. Nissen, *Eenzaamheid als zoeken naar God*, pp. 98–9.

can meet each other: 'Our principal endeavour and goal is to devote ourselves to the silence and solitude of the cell. This is holy ground, a place where, as a man with his friend, the Lord and his servant often speak together; there is the faithful soul frequently united with the Word of God; there is the bride made one with her spouse; there is earth joined to heaven, the divine to the human. The journey, however, is long, and the way dry and barren, that must be traversed to attain the fount of water, the land of promise.'[115]

Even Moses understood how long the journey to the Promised Land would be when he stood on the holy ground on the mountain Horeb (cf. Exod. 3). The journey of the Jewish people through the desert was indeed extremely difficult (cf. Exod. 12:29). Therefore the Carthusian statutes do not want to idealise or apotheosise the solitary life. On the contrary, the holy ground in the cell is above all desert ground. The encounter with God is never simple or easy! The solitary desert remains a place of encounter and abandonment. 'A storm in silence' is how solitary life is described by the Flemish former Carthusian Kris Wittevrongel: 'It is an ear-splitting silence which is not passive at all. In the cell, there is a lot of passion and struggle with demons and with God. The monk shares the experiences of biblical figures. The joyful inner peace of most old monks is not gained without sacrifices. They had a long and reckless life of searching.'[116]

---

[115] Statutes of the Carthusian order, 4.1.

[116] J. Vranckx, 'Ik was een kartuizer', *Gazet van Antwerpen*, 2–3 September 2006, pp. 4–5.

The Latin pun which is used by William of St Thierry in his *Golden Epistle* is not correct: he makes the wrong linguistic association of the words *cella* (cell) and *caelum* (heaven) by deriving both words from the Latin verb *celare* which means *to hide*. It is correct to do so for the word *cella*, but not for *caelum*. William's pun is also used by Denys the Carthusian:

> In the Latin, the written as well as the spoken text, there is a certain affinity between the words *cell* (*cella*) and *heaven* (*caelum*). We have already noted that solitary life in the cell is directed towards perfect union with God, an activity which will be perfect and complete in heaven. The *Golden Epistle* says that the words *heaven* and *cell* have a semantic affinity because they bear witness to the same spirit. Both words are derived from the Latin verb *to hide* (*celare*). Just like we shall *hide* in heaven, we *hide* in our cells. What we shall do in heaven, we do already in our cells. What does it mean? To be with God and to rejoice in God. Because we accomplish this activity in our cells with constancy and fidelity, I dare to say: the holy angels of God consider the cell as a kind of heaven and they enjoy being in the cell as much as they might enjoy heaven. When the cell becomes an uninterrupted performance of heavenly activities, cell and heaven will unite with each other … When the human spirit enters in prayer, it means that the soul leaves the body, the way from the

cell to heaven is not long, nor difficult. Heaven can be reached in the cell.[117]

The Dutch Carthusian Johan De Bruijn admits that most monks feel quite uneasy about this kind of interpretation. 'The reason for this displeasure is clear: the Latin translation literally eulogises the solitary monk, or even stronger "it catapults him into heaven" ... Of course solitude advances contemplation and brings humanity closer to its final destination, but in this case solitude is idealised, as is done quite often by those who have not experienced it for a longer time.'[118]

We want to repeat that in Bruno's mind, the solitary life was only an anticipation or an image of heavenly bliss and not an attainment or an achievement of it. Solitude is also experienced as frightening, abhorrent and oppressive in a cell. It can be like a prison or a dungeon, like a grave in which a monk feels buried alive, or even as a hell from which he wants to escape. Even after one single night in the Grande Chartreuse, the Dutch journalist Leo Fijen had a taste of this fundamental negative experience: 'I never had this experience in my life: it is quieter than quiet in here. Silence is written with capital letters. For the very first time I experience a silence more penetrating than the silence of the mountains. There is always some noise, but in here there is total silence. I am really alone ... I lie on my bed and I wonder about who lived in this cell, struggling with so many

---

[117] Denys Le Chartreux, *Eloge de la vie en solitude*, pp. 211–12.
[118] J. De Bruijn, *De Gulden Brief nog leesbaar?*, p. 121.

questions. How much disquiet, affliction, loneliness and abandonment was experienced in this cell? I understand that silence may be very menacing. I even understand that the confrontation with your own self may be very frightening because it is inevitable. If this isn't your vocation, you could become crazy and you might run away within twenty-four hours. Silence creeps into all your fibres and into each corner of your heart. You cannot escape. You have to remove all masks; jettison all illusions; adjust all expectations. There is no mirror on the wall, and yet you will meet your own image every second.'[119]

It is quite obvious that new candidates must experience the sometimes bitter taste of solitary life. The choice for Carthusian life does not endure idealism or euphemism. That is the reason why Guigo I was concerned about the realistic confrontation of new candidates with solitude. His concern for the novices was pragmatic as well as pedagogic:

> The hard and severe demands of our lifestyle must be revealed to each novice who chooses to embrace it. As far as possible, the humility and the stark nature of our life must be explained to him. If he still remains fearless and committed, and if he really wants to give up his love for all secular things, and if his bones choose death – a kind of death from which is said: 'If we die with Christ, than we shall live with Him' (Rom. 6:8) – if he promises with the greatest conviction to walk on the tough road because of the Lord, then we

[119]   L. Fijen, *De reis van je hoofd naar je hart*, pp. 136–7.

ask him – according to the Gospel – to reconcile first with those who have something against him and, if he should have damaged someone, to restore it (Matt. 5:24).

In the beginning the novice will be treated gently. He is not expected to observe immediately all the severities of our institution, but little by little, with the proper measure when reason or necessity reveal that moment.[120]

Just as every Carthusian monastery is built according to the same architectural pattern, every hermitage consists of the same typical structure of two floors and four rooms. On the ground floor is a store for firewood and a workroom with a bench. Because the cell is usually warmed with a cast-iron stove, each monk receives in spring a huge mass of wood as his provision for winter. A step leads to the first floor which contains two other spaces. The first room originally served as a kitchen, because the first Carthusians cooked most of their own meals each day. But this custom was abolished in the thirteenth century because it took too much time. Since then, this room has been established as the so-called *Ave Maria*: every time the monk enters this room, he kneels before the statute of the Virgin and he prays a Hail Mary.

The last room on the first floor is really the intimate heart of the cell. In the *cubiculum* or living room, the Carthusian monk prays, studies, eats and sleeps. He spends the greatest part of his day and of his life in this space. The massive

---

[120]   *Customs of Chartreuse*, 22, 1; 4.

wooden furniture is certainly the most remarkable element. It resembles an old-fashioned alcove with a bed on one side and an oratory with a pew on the other. When the bell rings, each monk kneels down in his private oratory to pray the different monastic offices.[121] During the weekdays all meals are taken in the cell. There is a table at the window, so that the monk can read a book or look outside while he is eating. Another table serves as a desk for study and *lectio divina*.[122] There is also a small basin for washing-up and for personal hygiene. Some monasteries even have a toilet with running water in the cells. Finally, each hermitage has a small walled garden and a covered gallery for physical comfort when it rains or snows. 'In comparison with other monastic orders, the Carthusian order has the advantage that a monk is free to organise his personal rhythm in the cell. He may cultivate flowers or vegetables in his garden, he may enjoy the surrounding nature, he may write poems or paint icons in his cell, and so on. Whoever is strong enough to endure solitude, will be very happy in here,'[123] notes the former Carthusian Kris Wittevrongel. Denys the Carthusian made a clear distinction between the activities a monk may perform in his cell:

> There are two kinds of activities which a monk may perform in his cell. The first activities are required and common. These are the activities prescribed

---

[121] This alcove does not exist in every Carthusian monastery: some just have beds and a pew to pray.
[122] *Lectio divina*: spiritual reading of the Bible. We will come back to this subject later on.
[123] J. Vranckx, *Ik was een kartuizer*, p. 5.

by our order and our statutes: praying the monastic offices; respecting silence; the strict regime of fasting; observing night watches and rejecting all vanities. All these exercises are accomplished at certain times and our common law forbids us to neglect them. The other exercises however are spontaneous and personal. They depend on individual possibilities and the conditions of place, time and customs. 'For not everything is good for everyone, and no one enjoys everything' (Sir. 37:28). What is beautiful for one may be ugly for another. The personal exercises may be quite different: study, lectures, transcription, meditation, prostration, sorrow, repentance. There are also more crude activities, deemed less sensible: manual labour, gardening, attentive service, etc. So everyone must do what he thinks he is able to do and what is the most fruitful for him. However, no one may do the same thing all the time. On the contrary, the angel revealed to St Anthony that he was to perform just as many spiritual as corporal exercises.[124]

While the hermitages in each Carthusian monastery are built according to the same model and look quite similar, there are some prominent differences. The cells and gardens in Serra San Bruno, Farneta (Tuscany, Italy) or Portes, for example, are large and ample in comparison with the Grande Chartreuse. These hermitages are real houses. Because of their southern look, the warm materials and the local flora

---

[124]   Denys le Chartreux, *La vie et la fin du solitaire*, p. 58.

in the gardens, the Italian hermitages seem even domestic and cosy. During a meeting with the Prior of Farneta in 2003, he emphasised the importance of space and ample room for sound psychological health, in order to reduce all negative feelings of imprisonment or captivity. The solitary monk needs a certain physical and psychological space within the walls of his cell to move freely. The hermitages and the gardens in the Grande Chartreuse are much smaller and poorer, even rudimentary. There is no flowing water and the monks must search for water in the cloister. Here, the more narrow the cell, the more intense the spiritual discipline and the psychological strength needed to endure the solitude and the silence that is encouraged.

In order to avoid all unnecessary breaks from the confinement of the cell, *The Customs of Chartreuse* contain a very detailed list of items which a Carthusian monk needs for daily routine and manual labour: bedclothes, kitchen utensils, tools, footwear, the number of garments, etc. Guigo's enumeration may seem exaggerated and even paternalistic or foolish. That is the reason why he asked explicitly not to ridicule his prescriptions: only those who know the solitary life from the inside will understand the logic of his reason.

Guigo's list of utensils also contains different kinds of writing materials and parchment. St Bruno had chosen the transcription of books as the main manual labour for the Carthusian monks, because it can be done without disturbing individual solitude. This act of transcribing is in fact an ancient custom of the Desert Fathers; for example St Jerome in the Palestinian desert. The Carthusian order did not have scriptoria like the Benedictine or Cistercian orders. Each hermit received enough writing materials and parchment to perform his task in his cell. The Carthusians monks considered the transcribing of books to be an apostolic service to the world, because written words are able to proclaim the faith and alert readers to error and sin. Denys the Carthusian says about the copying of books: 'Writing is the most noble form of all physical exercises. We, who cannot preach or teach with our mouths, we teach by books and we inspire our readers to preach.'[125]

Since the art of printing, the transcribing of books has fallen into abeyance. Other forms of manual labour were invented by the Carthusian monks. The monastery of Portes for example manufactures small wooden boxes for the packaging of the Chartreuse elixir. Guigo's list of utensils reads:

> The inhabitant of the cell receives a rough-weave straw mattress for his bed, a pillow, a cover or a blanket of thick sheepskin and a blanket of rough wool. As regards clothing: two penitent garments, two garments, two fur cloaks, one for daily use and one for occasional use, two habits, three pairs of socks, four pairs of footwear, some animal skins, a mantle, shoes for during the day and the night, grease to keep shoes supple, two lumbar belts and one belt made of rough hemp cords. The solitary monks may not complain about size or colour of bedclothes or garments. It is convenient that monks – and especially hermits – wear

---

[125]   Denys le Chartreux, *La vie et la fin du solitaire*, p. 59.

simple and worn clothes and use simple utensils. He receives also two needles, thread, a razor for his head, a whetstone and a leather belt to sharpen his tools.

To write: a secretary, a few plumes, some chalk, two pumices, two inkpots, a pen-knife, two scrubbing knives to smooth the surfaces of the parchment, an awl, a dust coat, a board to order sheets, a few basins and a peg. We teach each new candidate, as far as possible, the art of copying. However, when a monk practises an individual art which is not done in common, he receives all the tools he needs.

The inhabitant of the cell receives two books from the library. He treats them with precious care, so that the books do not become soiled from smoke, dust or other marks. We insist on the fact that all books are made and kept with the greatest care, as eternal food for our souls, because we can only preach God's Word by our hands and not with our mouths. As many books as we copy, so many times we serve as messengers of truth …

We prepare our own meals. For this reason each solitary monk receives two kettles, two bowls and a third for bread as well as a napkin. The fourth bowl must be large enough for washing-up. He also receives two spoons, a bread knife, a pot, a cup, a water pitcher, a saltshaker, a dish, two small bags in which to keep vegetables and a towel. For the cooking fire he receives kindling or tinder, a pan, a stock of firewood and an axe. And for manual labour a pick-axe. We ask the reader not to ridicule or to reject all this without having been in a cell for a long time, in this terrible cold and heavy snowfall. All these things are given to the monk in order that he does not have to leave the cell. More importantly he does not leave the cell except on occasions when the whole community gathers in the cloister or the church.[126]

The hermitages of the converse brothers are similar to those of the monks. They have a *cubiculum*, an *Ave Maria* and a workplace. In some Carthusian monasteries, the friars' cells are concentrated around the small cloister, but in other monasteries they have large rooms in a common building. Guigo I did not provide the converse brothers with writing materials for the copying of books, but with tools like spades, bores and shovels because they were responsible for the maintenance of the entire community. They received appropriate clothing, while they often had to work in the cold, snow and rain:

> The converse brothers have three garments, three pairs of socks, two pairs of slippers, shoes for during the day and during the night, a fur cloak, some animal skins, a cap, a pair of woollen gloves, two lumbar belts and a belt. Their shoes are made of cowhide ... They receive old animal skins and the fur cloaks, previously belonging to other monks. For their bed they receive a rough-weave straw mattress, a pillow and a blanket ... In the dormitory in the *higher house* they only have beds, fur cloaks and night slippers. All these things provide protection and cover against the cold. Their shoe laces

---

[126] *Customs of Chartreuse*, 28, 1–6.

and their belts are made of rough hemp, as are their lumbar belts. We decided all this so they may never yearn for vanity, only for that which is necessary and useful.

They receive also two bowls for edibles, and a piece of linen for covering their bread. A bigger bowl is provided for washing-up; a pot, a cup, a saltshaker, a spoon, a knife and a water pitcher. They also receive some tools: an axe, a pick-axe, a scythe, a billhook, two needles, thread and a bore ... The shepherds have woven gauze-like overalls, which they wear only to make cheese. We have given two small fur cloaks to our shepherds, which are made of two sheepskins. They only wear them when they are outside the boundaries of the 'desert' during the rainy season. During milking, wherever it takes place, they observe silence.[127]

The rhythm of life of the Carthusian monks

The monotony of time: through repetition towards deepening

A very specific yet unusual quality of the film *Into Great Silence* is its slow and repetitive rhythm. We are used to other cinematic genres: special effects and fast images. Even Cardinal Danneels noticed the unusual rhythm of the Carthusian film: 'The speed of monastic life is also the speed of the movie. Everything we see, takes the time that it takes in reality. The cutting of a piece of cloth for example, or

---

[127] *Customs of Chartreuse*, 57, 1–4; 61, 1–3.

the filling of a decanter with water. The life of a Carthusian monk exists in repetition: always the same prayers, the same schedule, the same rituals. Through repetition there is a deepening. This is the main quality of the film: the repetition of citations, the images of hands in a holy water font, the repetition of the same rituals ... One of the most magnificent qualities of the film is the experience of time or the experience of the seasons. For monks, who spent the greatest part of their lives in a cell where the sun only penetrates from May until September, the seasonal change is very important. Monastic experiences of time exist in the eternal repetition of the seasons.'[128]

'The external rhythm of our life is determined by the movement of the liturgical year, which coincides with the change of the seasons,' confirms a monk from the Grande Chartreuse. 'The seasons move through a large cycle of life: birth, growth, maturity, deterioration, death. The rough climate of the high mountains and the absence of modern amenities, which only neutralise the effect of the seasons, makes us very sensitive to the powers of the cosmos. So we are very lucky to live here. For the moment, life is determined by the hard winter, by snow and cold. Life among us has fallen asleep, the trees have lost their leaves, the cold cuts through. But one can feel the secret hope for new life. It only waits for a glimpse of the sun to reveal itself in the joyful song of birds who had disappeared and in the noise

---

[128]   M. De Roeck, *Kardinaal Danneels over Into Great Silence*, p. 2.

of swollen rivers brought to life by the melting of the snow. Spring is in the air! Life awakes!'[129]

The daily rhythm of the Carthusian monks exists in the permanent interruption of activities and occupation in the cell by the praying of the monastic offices. When the bell rings, each monk kneels down in his private oratory to sing the office. Just three times a day the community gathers in the church: at midnight for night office, in the morning for Mass and in the late afternoon for Vespers. The entire office – except Prime and Compline – is only sung in community on Sundays and feast days.

This repetitive timetable may seem quite boring to outsiders, but for the Carthusian monks this rhythm renders inner peace and spiritual freedom. New candidates always need an ordered structure, lest they become lost in useless reverie in their cells. Little by little the monk must learn to live the external rule as an inner rule and not as an institutional duty. He must learn to organise his different activities and occupations in the cell in a way that brings as much spiritual benefit as possible. The fragmentation of different activities prevents the monk risking being fanatical about just one activity! That is why each activity is limited, even sleep. Denys the Carthusian observes:

> Some exercises in the cell are obligatory, as well as the times in which they must be completed. Some of these exercises are spiritual, others corporal. The spiritual exercises consist in praying the offices (the office of

---

the day and of the deceased), the celebration of the Eucharist, etc. The corporal activities consist in taking care of the body, ensuring rest, clothing and eating his meals. Wearing the penitential belt, abstinence and a hard bed fall between spiritual and corporal exercises. Other exercises are not obligatory or prescribed. Some of these exercises are very fruitful because they happen spontaneously – these are spiritual, like meditation, prayer, love for God, supplications, singing of hymns, study and lectures. Others are corporal, extra fastening, abstinence, castigation and night watch. The obligatory exercises, corporal as well as spiritual, must be accomplished at the prescribed hours and times …

For the rest, the solitary monk must fill his days with the praying of psalms and liturgical prayers, the praise of God, meditation and ardent contemplation … At least once a day, on a certain hour, he must consider with devotion the Passion of Christ and examine his conscience. Whoever is strong and ardent may pray the entire psalter at separate times each day. This is a very fruitful use of time, especially when it is done with devotion and quiet so that the atmosphere of each psalm comes alive … At last, I confirm that a solitary monk who lives as I have described will grow each day in holy love, in salutary wisdom, in inner fruitfulness, in divine assistance, in spiritual purity, in the denial of the world and of the flesh. He will learn to enjoy the divine Presence, by the peaceful union of his heart with God's heart. He will pray the psalms and waken without any interruption, he will feel at ease, he will become more peaceful and more desiring without any satisfaction.[130]

'The most fundamental occupation of an inhabitant of a cell is the Lord,' remarks another Carthusian monk. 'This *unum necessarium* or this single occupation is evident in different spiritual, intellectual and material practices. A single piece of music is played differently on different instruments in an orchestra. The monk is a man of one single piece: one in essence and one in action. He achieves unity because he directs all occupations to one single goal: the purity of heart and love. All the rest is a pure waste, pointless and simply for appearance sake.'[131]

In order to understand the repetitive and monotonous rhythm of the Carthusian daily life, we take a look at the horarium of the Grande Chartreuse:

Schedule of the cloistered monks		Schedule of the converse brothers	
6.30:	Rise	6.00:	Rise
7.00:	Prime and silent prayer in the cell		Prime and silent prayer in the cell
8.00:	Community Mass and private Mass in a chapel (or after Vespers)	8.00:	Community Mass
		9.15:	Terce in the cell
		9.30:	Work in the ateliers or outside
10.00:	Terce, study and work in the cell		

---

[130]   Denys le Chartreux, *Eloge de la vie en solitude*, pp. 184–6.
[131]   *Paroles de chartreux*, p. 175.

Schedule of the cloistered monks	Schedule of the converse brothers
12.00: Sext, lunch and rest in the cell	12.00: Sext, lunch and rest in the cell
	13.30: None in the cell
	13.45: Work in the ateliers or outside
14.00: None, study and work in the cell	
17.00: Vespers in church	17.00: Vespers in church
17.45: Dinner in the cell	17.45: Dinner in the cell
18.15: Silent prayer in the cell	18.15: Silent prayer and lecture in the cell
18.45: Compline in the cell Sleep	18.45: Compline in the cell Sleep
23.30: Rise	
Matins of the Virgin in the cell	0.00: Rise
0.15: Matins and Lauds in church	0.15: Matins in the church
	1.45: Silent prayer in the cell Sleep
2.30: Matins of the Virgin in the cell Sleep	

There are some notable differences between the schedule of the cloistered monks and the schedule of the converse brothers: the friars have fewer moments of solitude in the cell and they have more manual labour outside the cell. We already indicated that the friars are responsible for the maintenance and all material responsibilities of the community. The schedule of the Grande Chartreuse is quite uniform throughout Carthusian monasteries across the world, male and female communities alike, with a few exceptions. In the age of Guigo I the schedule was more dependent on the change of the seasons. However, the actual schedule is in fact quite similar to the daily rhythm of the first Carthusian monks in the high mountains of Chartreuse. In *The Customs of Chartreuse* these provisions about time are stated:

> Unless on feasts ... and during the weeks of Christmas, Easter and Pentecost, the evening Office of the church is preceded by a considerable period of personal prayer in the cell until the bell rings. This moment of prayer extends from ides[132] in September until calends in November. This period of time must be long enough to pray fifty psalms at ease. From the calends in November until the calends in February, this period of time remains unchanged. From then until Easter, this period of time is shortened, but still long enough to pray the Matins of Our Lady. From Easter until the ides of September, the length of this period remains unchanged.
>
> When the bell rings for the second time, we hasten to the church and try to arrive before the third ring. When the prior or his appointee gives a sign, we kneel down and we pray the Our Father with earnest and with devotion three times. At all other times we only pray one Our Father. Then we rise and with respect we pray the psalms.

---

[132] Ides and calends are ancient time indications on the Roman calendar. The ides is the thirteenth day of the month; calends is the first day of the month.

After we have sung Matins, we have a short interval in which to pray the seven penitential psalms. Then we pray Lauds. From the calends in October until Easter, Lauds ends at dawn. After Easter they start on this moment. We never return to our beds after Matins! After the same calends until Easter, Prime begins at dawn; afterwards we pray Prime at sunrise … The period between Prime and Terce in winter, and the period between Matins and Prime in summer, is devoted to spiritual exercises. The period between Terce and Sext in winter, and the period between Prime and Terce in summer, is devoted to manual labour. But labour must always be interrupted by short moments of prayer … In summer, the period between Sext and None is devoted to a short rest. The period between None and Vespers is for manual labour. It is always permitted to interrupt labour for a short moment of prayer or supplication. From Vespers until Compline, all activities are directed to the spiritual exercises.

When the bell rings for Compline, we consider this: the bell is rung at a time when there is still enough light to read.[133] After Compline we pray the Our Father three times and we hasten to our beds. It is not only advised, but even required to take care of sleep during the periods which are devoted to rest. It helps us to stay awake during the rest of the day. Usually we pray Matins and Vespers in the church. Compline

---

[133]   There was no electricity in Guigo's age of course.

however, is prayed in the cell. Only on feasts, vigils and memorials do we gather in the church.[134]

Solitude and communion: Carthusian moments of encounter

The Carthusians are not hermits in the strict sense of the word. They are solitary monks who share a minimum of community life, mainly on Sundays and feasts. The observance of solitude is abrogated for the greatest part by intense moments of fraternal encounter and consolation. All liturgical offices, except Prime and Compline, take place in the church and the Eucharist is concelebrated by all priests, in contrast to the rest of the week. Even lunch is taken together in the refectory. According to the ancient monastic customs, silence is preserved during lunch. An inspirational book, the statutes of the order or an article is read aloud by one of the monks.

In the refectory in Serra San Bruno, a simple plate above the Prior's seat commemorates the visit of Pope John Paul II on 5 October 1984. A remarkable anecdote came to life during the papal lunch with the Carthusian monks, so Prior Jacques Dupont tells us, with a spirit of childish joy. While the papal letter on the occasion of the nine hundredth anniversary of the foundation of the Carthusian order (14 May 1984) was being read aloud, John Paul II knocked on the table to interrupt the reading while saying: 'I would like to hear if the monks are still able to speak after all those years.' The surprised monks didn't know how to react and they continued eating in silence. That day, only the Pope and

---

[134]   *Customs of Chartreuse*, 29, 1–6.

the Prior,[135] who sat near him, had a conversation during dinner!

On most Sundays and feasts, chapter reunion is kept. Chapter is a very important institution within the Carthusian order, because the prior addresses all necessary communications which interest the whole community. The names of the deceased monks and converses are read aloud and the saints are commemorated. All official meetings of the community are held in the chapter hall, for example the vote on the entry of new candidates and novices.

Another important moment of communion and encounter is recreation on Sunday afternoons, which lasts one and a half to two hours. The monks chat and talk with each other, they discuss issues or they make jokes. In summer, recreation is held in the open air to extend the sense of relaxation. The weekly walk on Monday afternoons, which is called *spaciement* in Carthusian jargon, is certainly the most striking activity. For three or even four hours, the Carthusian monks walk two by two in the broad areas surrounding the monastery. In the film *Into Great Silence* they gambol through the snow like playful schoolboys and slide rambunctiously down the white flanks. It is the relaxed companionship of brothers. These moments of physical activity are a very important element within the Carthusian tradition, because they create the necessary psychological balance – sometimes even an escape – for the many hours of solitude in the cell.

---

[135] The Prior was Dom Pierre-Marie Anquez (d. 2012), the founder of a Carthusian monastery in Brazil.

The necessity of the weekly walk is described as follows in the statutes of the order:

> Since, as St Bruno says, when wearied by our quite austere rule and application to spiritual things, our rather delicate natures can often be refreshed and renewed by the charms and beauties of woods and countryside. The fathers have a walk every week – with the exception of Holy Week … Our walks should be such as to further brotherly union and also the spiritual progress of our souls. Hence all are to walk together, taking the same route so that each one can, in turn, talk with the others – unless, for a reasonable cause, it seems better to have two or three groups. Should it be necessary to go through a town or village, they will be content simply to pass through, preserving due decorum, and never entering the houses of seculars. They should not hold conversation with strangers, nor give them anything. On the walks, we are not to eat or drink anything, except plain water, found by the wayside. These conversations together are intended to help us to grow in mutual love, and to moderate somewhat our solitude. Let us be on our guard against talking excessively, or shouting, or indulging in indecorous laughter. Let our conversations be religious, not frivolous or worldly; let us shun any semblance of detraction or murmuring. Should a difference of opinion arise, let us know how to listen

and to see the matter from the other's point of view so that in all things the bond of mutual love will grow ever stronger.[136]

Once or sometimes even twice a year there is the so-called *grand spaciement*: a *great walk* with a picnic. With strong walking shoes, a hat and a walking-stick, the community leaves for an entire day. Most great walks take place in the forests, the mountains or the fields of another region, but sometimes an excursion to a pilgrimage place or a historic site is organised. For these occasion cars or a minibus are borrowed or rented. A film crew from the Italian television once followed the community of Serra San Bruno during the *gran'spaziamento* to the famous byzantine church of La Cattolica in Stilo on the east coast of Calabria. The images of praying hermits gathered under the robust domes of the tenth-century chapel, where once the hymns of Greek Orthodox monks resounded, are quite moving. Even during moments of relaxation, the Carthusians remain faithful to their contemplative vocation.

Unlike the monks, the Carthusian converses have no moments of encounter and consolation on Sundays and feasts, but conversely a stricter observance of solitude and silence. As a compensation for the many hours of manual labour and care for the community, the friars withdraw on Sunday to their cells for prayer and rest. Of course they assist at all liturgical offices and Mass in the church, as well as at the common dinner in the refectory and the encounter in

---

[136]   Statutes of the Carthusian order, 3.22.

the chapter hall, but they do not participate at recreation in the afternoon. Even most Mondays they stay at home. They only have one single walk during the month, mostly together with the monks. The friars are indeed real Carthusians and they have a vocation for the solitary life. Therefore, each month a day of complete solitude is observed and each year a silent retreat of eight days.

Asceticism and poverty within the Carthusian order

Fasting and abstinence: purification of body and spirit

'Christ suffered for us, leaving us an example, that we should follow in his steps; this we do by accepting the hardships and anxieties of this life, by embracing poverty with the freedom of God's sons, and by renouncing our own will. Moreover, in accordance with monastic tradition it is for us also to follow Christ in his fast in the desert, treating the body hard and making it obey us, so that the mind may flame with longing for God.'[137] These words begin the chapter on fasting and abstinence in the statutes of the order. A spirit of poverty and asceticism really belongs in the foundations of Carthusian spirituality. 'He rather lived poor for Christ than rich for the world' is written on the death roll of St Bruno. However, the Carthusians never understood poverty in the same way as the mendicant orders did, for example the Franciscans or the Dominicans. The *numerus clausus* of 13 monks and 16 converses was

---

[137] Statutes of the Carthusian order, 1.7.

introduced by Guigo I as a means to stop begging. Material poverty and corporal asceticism are largely directed to the sense of inner purification and spiritual susceptibility in the Carthusian tradition. The solitary monk must direct his heart to communion with God and he must try to avoid everything which impedes this unity: all desires which arise from material things and from the flesh. 'In God exists all perfect, beautiful and desirable qualities,'" wrote Denys the Carthusian. 'That is why we may not desire, tolerate or search for realities other than God alone and even those things which bring, lead and direct us to God. We must reject with care all consolation, beauty and pleasure and we must turn away from what separates and distracts our soul from the contemplation of God.'[138]

A monastic withdrawal from the world automatically includes abstinence and sacrifice. The Carthusian life is rudimentary as regards human comfort and temperate regarding culinary arts. It can take years to adapt physically and mentally to the regime of asceticism, fasting and interrupted sleep. When the (new) monk is alone in his cell, temptations like hunger, sleep or the need for human contact and/or comfort may be very strong. It is not surprising that most candidates leave the monastery after a few years, months or even days, because they cannot overcome their physical or mental limits. For this reason the statutes of the order recommend prudence and calm at the beginning of monastic life. Dom Marcellin Theeuwes had to grit his teeth

---

[138] Denys le Chartreux, 'Cordiale sive praecordiale', in C. Bagonneua, *Chroniques de l'extase*, p. 41.

during the novitiate before his body and mind could adapt to the Carthusian regime: 'It cost me blood, tears and sweat! The first three years I was wondering: why did I leave the Cistercian order? You feel the need to compare and you become the toy of your own impulses and tendencies. This period was a real test from God, however I did not have this feeling. I suffered physically, I was even nauseous. I was sick quite often. I had fevers, sometimes for several days. During the first year and a half, every two months – almost like clockwork – I had nightmares. The same scenario was repeated over and over. I was thinking: I am sick, I shall have to return to the Cistercians! Then the bad dreams disappeared, without any trace. On that particular day, I was able to take a real step.'[139]

The regime of fasting in the Carthusian order consists of total abstinence from meat, a lunch of water and dry bread each Friday (originally also on Monday and Wednesday), abstaining from all dairy products, cheese, butter and milk during Advent and Lent. In addition during the long monastic Lent from 14 September, the feast of the Exaltation of the Cross, until Easter, there is only one meal a day and a small snack for dinner. Moreover there is never breakfast. However, the vegetarian diet is very healthy and generous: vegetables, potatoes, fruits, fish, eggs, bread, pasta, rice and even wine, beer or cider. Lunch consists of three dishes: soup, a warm meal and dessert, mostly fruit. Due to the amount of hard physical labour, the converses

---

139   J. Reijnders, *Een reis in stilte*, p. 82.

receive more food than the monks. They have breakfast each morning.

Fasting and abstinence is not a matter of heroic or Spartan living. The Carthusian monks do not consider themselves as pre-eminent 'giants' among the ascetics. Fasting and abstinence do not break the human body, nor undermine physical health. This observance affects the body, but it does not wound, hurt or kill the body. A sick body can affect the mind, and a sick mind is no longer transparent or sensitive enough for contemplation and prayer. 'The narrowness of the cell tires the head,' wrote Bernard from Portes in his letter to a recluse. 'It is a fact that regular fasting has the same effect. Abstinence which is too severe bears no fruit ... Regular eating, drinking and sleeping are good ingredients for a healthy lifestyle. They are also fruitful for the purity of heart and body ... A moderate lifestyle is pleasing to God and more useful for soundness of body and mind. It is more beneficial to the body, than excessive food following a period of severe fasting.'[140]

Accordingly, *The Customs of Chartreuse* and many general chapters emphasise the necessity of a moderate asceticism and forbid supplementary abstinences and sacrifices. The ancient use of the so-called days of blood-letting or blood diminutions, from the Latin verb *minuere* (to diminish), must be seen in this philosophy: five times a year – four times for the converse brothers – a diminution of the discipline

---

[140] Bernard De Portes, *Lettre au Reclus Raynaud*, pp. 61–3.

was allowed over three days.[141] To take care of their physical health, the Carthusians had permission to eat more and to sleep longer, they drank wine at dinner and they had the right to make their complaints to the cook! In other words, fasting and abstinence must always remain reasonable and responsible. In *The Customs of Chartreuse* and the statutes of the order the following prescriptions are made:

> Without the permission or knowledge of the Prior nobody is allowed to perform supplementary abstinences, castigations, awakes or other devotional exercises than those which are prescribed. And when the Prior commands someone supplementary food, sleep, or whatever, or if he wants to dictate a more severe measure or penance, it is forbidden to refuse.[142]

> We should practise mortification of the flesh not merely out of obedience to the statutes, but primarily to be freed from the tendencies of our lower nature and enabled to follow the Lord more readily and cheerfully. But if, in a particular case, or with the passage of time, someone finds that any of the aforesaid observances is beyond his strength, and that he is hindered rather than helped in the following of Christ, let him, in a filial spirit, arrange some suitable measure of relaxation

---

[141] Blood-letting was a common medical custom in the Middle Ages, based on the ancient Greek doctrine about lifeblood. An artery was opened to let flow some blood as a cure against diseases or ailments. The practice of blood-letting was painful and unpleasant. That's why most monastic rules permitted certain relaxations during the days of blood diminutions. Only in 1373 was this custom abrogated in the Carthusian order.

[142] *Customs of Chartreuse*, 35, 1–2.

with the Prior, at least for a time. But, ever mindful of Christ who calls, let him see what he can do; and what he is unable to give to God by common observance, let him offer in some other way, denying himself and taking up his cross daily ... Novices, therefore, should be accustomed gradually to the fasts and abstinences of the Order, so that, under the guidance of the novice master, they may prudently and safely tend towards the rigour of complete observance. He should teach them to be especially watchful not to make future fasting a pretext for over-indulgence at meals.[143]

Denys the Carthusian agreed on the fact that fasting and abstinence are an essential part of Carthusian spirituality. Gluttony and abundance aggravate the human body and confuse the mind, moderation and temperance on the other hand relieve them. 'Without temperance, no spiritual reform' is one of the quotes of the Desert Father John Cassian (d. 435) used by Denys the Carthusian in his treatise *The Food and the Table of the Solitary Monk*:

The Apostle says: 'I strike a blow to my body and make it my slave' (1 Cor. 9:27). Keeping moderation in food is very difficult. However, it is useful and necessary to do so, because it is impossible to reach divine perfection without moderation. Whoever enjoys abundant and copious eating and drinking will no longer remain attentive during night watch, nor pure during prayer, nor concentrate during meditation.

---

[143]   Statutes of the Carthusian order, 1.7.

John Cassian says: without attentive temperance, no spiritual reform will be reached. In the beginning it is useful to moderate a certain amount of food. The head will not be befogged, the senses will not be pinched and sleepiness will not be urged. That is why the Lord says: 'Be careful, or your hearts will be weighed down with carousing and drunkenness.' You do not have to weigh or measure the right amount of food on your plate or in your cup. Above all, use your experience and good sense to estimate your natural need for food. Do not eat to excess when the cup is full or when the food tastes well. To synthesise the remarks on food: be careful but detached when preparing meals, otherwise you will find more pleasure in the joy of eating than in the need for food.[144]

Denys the Carthusian once wrote in one of his other treatises on fasting and abstinence:

We are so unhappy! We strayed from the customs of the Fathers. We are not worthy to be called their sons. We fail in simplicity, poverty and abstinence. The hermits of the ancient *skete*[145] only ate once a week: fresh bread and water were a feast for them. If they received some fruits, it was considered a banquet. Human weakness however was accommodated in the century of St Benedict: 'We believe that for the daily meal, two kinds

---

[144] Denys le Chartreux, *La vie et la fin du solitaire*, pp. 43–4.
[145] A *skete* was a group of hermits in the primitive Church. The word *skete* comes from the Greek for asceticism.

of cooked food are sufficient at all meals; so that he who perchance cannot eat of one, may make his meal of the other' (*Rule of St Benedict,* chapter 39). St Augustine writes in his Rule: 'Restrain your body by abstinences which your health may endure. Aside from the meals, nobody is to eat, unless someone is sick.' Our ancient statutes prescribe: 'Herbs are never used to prepare the daily meals, except for some salt. It is only permitted to add something else out of pity. No one may have oil in his cell. On Monday, Wednesday and Friday we are satisfied with some bread and salt.' ... The solitary monk who eats alone in his cell must be equally humble and modest as he is in the refectory. If not, he fears men more than God and the angels. Finally we want to remind you of the evil which is sown by gluttony: gossip, apathy, sleepiness, bad mood, excess, waste of time, wilfulness, loss of true joy, insensibility and so many other sentiments. In order to avoid all these bad things, we must avoid hate, defeat gluttony and aspire to healthy moderation. St Benedict says: 'For nothing is so contrary to Christians as excess, as the Lord said: "Be on guard, so that your hearts will not be weighed down with dissipation and drunkenness and the worries of life" (Luke 21:34).'[146]

Poverty and simplicity: purification of greed and vanity

Unlike St Bruno who accepted fields, orchards and other donations from the local Calabrian aristocracy, Guigo

---

[146] Denys le Chartreux, *Eloge de la vie en solitude*, pp. 186–9.

I limited the common property of the Carthusian order. Wealth easily leads to greed, possessions which bring all kinds of material concerns and the hazards of the outside world. That's why Guigo I defined the limits of the territory of the Grande Chartreuse. As noted earlier, no possessions were allowed outside the 'borders' of the desert: no fields, no vines, no buildings, no tithes or donations for worship. The exploitation of the domain and the administration of the sacraments were not the main activities of the Carthusian community, as was the custom in most other monastic orders. The self-financing economic system and the number of 13 monks and 16 converses was to ensure the climate of privation, solitude and silence. The restriction of properties is defined as follows in *The Customs of Chartreuse*:

> With the help of God we protect ourselves and those who come after us against the temptation of greed. With this writing we define that the inhabitants of this place may have no possessions outside the boundary of the desert. This means: no fields, no orchards, no gardens, no churches, no cemeteries, no stipends, no tithes or anything of this kind.
>
> … We have heard – and we disagree with those religious who are seduced by abundant meals and the donations given by benefactors for the celebration of Masses for the deceased. This custom puts at risk all abstinences and it transforms prayers into merchandise, because there are as many banquets as there are Masses. When the prescriptions about fasting and prayer are not followed with a spirit of devotion, but depend only on occasional visitors who give food, they will not

last. There will be no day without a banquet or without a Mass, unless the donors of food do not appear. We will not entertain further discussion with those who think that these customs are commendable. Each may do whatever he thinks is good: he shall render account to God who knows our heart and innermost being. God will judge each person according to his behaviour and the fruits of his work.[147]

In the Carthusian tradition, poverty consists not only in the restriction of common property, but also the renunciation of personal possessions and economic solidarity among the different monasteries of the order. The emphasis on poverty is prominent in *The Customs of Chartreuse*, as well as in the decisions of most general chapters. Abuses and aberrations in certain monasteries were always condemned subsequently and restoration in the spirit of tradition was made. The general chapter of 1506, for example, prohibited the use of locks on the doors of the hermitages, because a cell is not the personal property of a monk, and therefore a key is of no use. However, while some historic Carthusian monasteries in Southern Europe (Spain, Italy, France) look rather like baroque palaces and cathedrals, the concrete poverty of the solitary monks remained quite unchanged in the cells. *Cartusia numquam deformata* – 'Carthusians have never been reformed because they have never been deformed', as the ancient adage says. Dom Jacques Dupont made a striking remark during our visit at the Charterhouse

---

[147] *Customs of Chartreuse*, 41, 1; 4.

of Serra San Bruno: 'The French Revolution was a blessing for the order. We were too rich!'[148]

The renunciation of secular possessions and properties, of comfort and pleasure, is one of the fundamental pillars of Carthusian spirituality. Instead of the satisfaction of secular and corporal needs, the solitary monk must focus his spirit on the eschatological accomplishment of all human happiness. For this reason, the use of material goods is reduced to a strict and merely functional minimum. This basic rule includes the use of modern communication like telephone, computer and internet.[149] The Carthusian monks try to live the vow of poverty according to its authentic significance in the Gospel: they deprive themselves of secular and temporal comforts and strive for divine and eternal realities. The statutes of the order note that 'the monk has elected to follow Christ in his poverty and by this poverty to be enriched. Depending on God and in no way wise on things terrestrial, he has treasure in heaven and it is there that his heart ever tends.'[150] *Paupertas* (poverty), *simplicitas* (moderation) and *rusticitas* (simplicity) are fundamental pillars of the spiritual architecture of the Carthusian order. The statutes explain the proper significance of the vow of poverty:

---

[148] Encounter with the Prior of Serra San Bruno on 17 August 2006.

[149] The Carthusian priors and procurators (economists) may use the internet and email for functional and necessary contacts. The general chapter of the Congregation of the Camaldolese Hermits of Monte Corona, however, banned all use of internet and email, even by the priors of the hermitages, in 2012.

[150] Statutes of the Carthusian order, 3.28.

Those who are solemnly professed are to have nothing but what the Order concedes to them for simple use. They have given up the right to ask or receive from another or to make gifts or of transfer of ownership without permission. Even amongst ourselves we cannot exchange or receive anything whatever without permission. While those in temporary vows and donates retain ownership of their property and the power to acquire more, they should not keep anything personal for themselves as is also the case for novices. Let the novice master inspire his newcomers with a singular love for poverty and a deep sense of separation from temporal goods and comforts.

In accordance with the counsels of Guigo if a garment or something of that sort be sent as a gift to one of the monks by a friend or relative let it be given not to him but rather to someone else, lest it seem to belong to him. Hence let no member of the Order claim a right of use or any other right in reference to books or to anything else which the Order may have received on his behalf; but if that use be granted to him, let him receive it with gratitude, clearly understanding that it belongs not to him but to others. No one is ever to have money under his control or in his possession. Since the Son of Man had nowhere to lay his head, let poverty and simplicity be strictly observed in our cells. Let us be constantly vigilant that there be nothing there that is superfluous or over-ornate – always willing to seek the opinion of the Prior in this matter.

Whoever is temporarily replacing another under obedience may not change anything whatsoever therein without permission. Moreover, the monks themselves are not to change or install anything in their cells, under obedience, without first submitting it to the Prior and obtaining his permission.[151]

Apathy and perseverance: a dialectic tension

Acedia, or apathy, in solitary life

A description of the monastic ideal of St Bruno and the spirituality of the Carthusian order could easily lead to all kinds of abstract, mystical or pious speculations. But Carthusian monks – and all contemplatives and religious – are no angels or heavenly creatures! They are human seekers of God, people searching for happiness and peace – as do we all! When monastic life is defined as an anticipation of eternal happiness, it does not mean that all contemplatives achieve and realise this eternal happiness here and now. The first to reject all kinds of idealising or romanticising of contemplative life are the contemplatives themselves. Dom Johan De Bruijn speaks about the afflictions and struggles which stability in a cell entails: 'aridity, monotony, confrontation with your own self and the traditional *thoughts* (making plans, desires, images, etc. which cross the human mind constantly), the emptiness of heart, mind and senses, the lack of external means of remaining motivated or the possibility of taking respite from the daily regimen. It is quite easy to peter out in routine or to escape in daydreams.

---

[151]   Statutes of the Carthusian order, 3.28.

The cell is the place where a man appears as a question mark for himself! Solitude constantly invites us to question our own faith and our images of God. Solitude is a constant provocation of the mystery of one's personality. Pope Paul VI once called monks the *experts of the invisible*, but they are even experts in the experience of night and waiting for God, with open hands.'[152]

It is obvious that the spirit and the original fervour may get lost in contemplative life and God may be experienced as absent. Dom Marcellin Theeuwes says that 'the solitary monk must step through the dark tunnel of faith. He knows that God is present, but quite often he becomes insensitive to God's presence. This feeling of absence may endure for a very long period and even lead to fundamental doubts. The monk may think he is able to live without God when confronted with his own human fragility. He cannot minimalise this reality in his spiritual life. Some saints use the image of an abyss – this expression is very accurate. The monk's fidelity is tested to the limit.'[153]

'It may look strange,' witnesses another Carthusian monk, 'but the most difficult part of our lives, the greatest struggle of each monk, is prayer. This is the reality of our lives, lives which are never perfect. Prayer must grow and mature slowly. Prayer becomes for the monk a mirror and measure of his purpose in life. The monk may never think that he knows how to pray, or that he has discovered the proper manner or technique. He must beg: "Lord, teach me how to

---

[152]   J. De Bruijn, *De Gulden Brief nog leesbaar?*, pp. 121–2.
[153]   S. Pruvot, *Entretien avec dom Marcellin*, p. 14.

pray." It is a permanent struggle. The monk will learn how to fight all enemies during prayer. He must fight all kinds of thoughts, distractions and desires which appear in his heart. This struggle is difficult. But when it seems impossible to pray or when his love for God or others weakens, he will feel the love of God. The Virgin Mary teaches us that the best school for prayer is prayer for others.'[154]

This experience of spiritual darkness, absence of aridity is called acedia in monastic jargon. The Latin word *acedia* comes from the Greek *akedia*, which means apathy or aversion. The Catechism of the Catholic Church speaks even about *laziness* or *indolence* in spiritual life: 'a form of depression due to lax ascetical practice, decreasing vigilance, carelessness of heart'.[155] The famous Egyptian Desert Father Evagrius Ponticus (d. 399) uses the word acedia to name the hermit's apathy during prayer: the inevitable confrontation with indifference, distraction, fatigue, lack of spirit and perseverance, melancholy, sadness, boredom and even aversion to the spiritual life. Evagrius also calls the feeling of acedia the *devil of midday*: midday is the usual time for boredom, fatigue and sleep. Solitude and prayer seem unbearable, exhausting and never-ending. The human mind begins to daydream about interesting and better places; or with nostalgia about family, the past and the future – all those lonely years in a cell seem frightening. 'The "devil" of acedia, also called the devil of midday, is the most difficult to endure,' writes Evagrius. 'He attacks the monk around

---

154   I Monaci di Serra San Bruno, *Sentieri del deserto*, p. 66.
155   *Catechism of the Catholic Church*, 2733; cf. 2094.

the fourth hour and he settles in his soul until the eighth hour ... The devil directs the monk's eyes constantly to the windows of the cell and he forces him to jump out ... Moreover, he whispers to him to hate the place in which he lives and to hate the state of life he has chosen ... The devil tries to lead him to another place by saying: "God can be worshipped everywhere." The devil will use every means to lead the monk out of his cell and to escape from his chosen state of life. Once the devil disappears, no other will take his place: a peaceful rest and an inexpressible joy will overflow in his soul after the battle.'[156]

The first step in the process of leaving the solitary life is set when the monk is tempted to escape from his cell. The 'external instability', says Evagrius Ponticus, is a sign of *an inner instability*. There is a distinct link between the monk's physical presence in the cell on the one hand and his spiritual discipline on the other. The most effective means to counter acedia is perseverance: to resist each temptation to leave the cell. Evagrius writes: 'To remain faithful in the cell, to be content and to resist, these are the essential foundations of ancient monasticism. The passion of the beginning must be refined by the toughest obstacle of all: time.'[157]

However, the word acedia does not appear literally in the writings of the primitive Carthusian tradition. The Carthusian monks knew this feeling through personal experience. In the early literature of the order, acedia is defined by terms such as 'desires' and 'spiritual vices': deep

---

[156]   Evagrius Ponticus, *Traité Pratique* II (SC 171), pp. 512–27.
[157]   Evagrius Ponticus, *Traité Pratique* II (SC 171), pp. 56–5.

feelings of sadness, confusion, apathy or even weariness of life. A longstanding solitude always implies a certain level of self-confrontation. This is so strong that it can lead to a real depression or a mental crisis. 'In the secrecy of the cell, the monk is tried by his own freedom and by his own limits. He is all alone and he must manage time and silent meditation. In his physical isolation, memories, fantasies and thoughts will cross his mind ... Different documents, manuals and instructions for novices and even interventions during general chapters speak of a *dark zone* in which the monk stands all alone. A novice master once wrote: "Solitude, and especially isolation, suppress most human relations. They lock us into our own limitations. Our activities are reduced to a minimum. The result is that we who are less distracted by sorrows than others are tempted to become quiet introverts. This is the real danger of solitude!" The physical and social isolation ... awaken all kinds of thoughts, memories and fantasies which disturb contemplation and amplify personal suffering. Solitude may become a real enemy.'[158] This mental state 'reinforces all sorts of sufferings, especially those of a psychological nature. It is not so difficult to understand that it is extremely painful to be separated from one's beloved. The first days of solitary life are a real temptation. Solitude awakes a *certain nostalgia*, which may be defined as a *nostalgia for oneself*. It is a much stronger emotion than any other kind of nostalgia, because it touches the deepest essence of our own being. Everything that makes life meaningful is over and will never return. The Carthusian life has only one

---

[158]   N. Nabert, *Tristesse, acédie et médecine des âmes*, p. 146.

single goal: to reach God.'[159] Denys the Carthusian writes about the struggle of the solitary monk with acedia in the following words:

> *Acedia* means a slackening or a weakening of the strength of the soul. The spirit is derailed and the inner vigilance disappears. An aversion for spiritual exercises occurs: the spirit is no longer able to fulfil virtuous exercises, or even worse – it fears them. In essence it is a kind of anaesthesia for these things, even an aversion for religious life. Acedia will end in the longer term in a real hatred for the monastic life which one has chosen. Acedia is an advocate for all hedonistic things: it tempts the heart with the charm of transient wealth, of pleasure, ambition and the power that comes with money ... Acedia may grow and flourish and dominate a person completely. The divine prescriptions and the rules of religious life will appear useless and merciless. A person may think and dare to say that God is insensitive, unkind, too severe and demanding and expecting the impossible!
>
> ... Acedia even attacks prayer, because it renders a praying person disobedient, feeble, slow and negligent in fighting apathy and distraction ... A careful monk will not encounter acedia, because he is not tempted by it and he rejects it. He has control over his senses and strives for inner peace and spiritual fulfilment. He refuses all sensible and external things to reach God. In

---

[159] Un Chartreux, 'Solitude et sainteté', *La Vie spirituelle*, pp. 146–47.

coenobitic life, acedia is fight: the religious fight against
and destroy acedia through the exchange of exercises,
admonitions, encouragements and stimulations. In
solitary life, acedia is always present and it does not
stop tempting the solitary monk. It only leaves him
when he dies, but before his death it will struggle and
fight him each day. That is the reason why our Fathers
write about the strong temptation of acedia in solitary
life: a solitary monk is not stimulated, encouraged or
observed by others. He enjoys a much larger freedom
than monks who live in community. The predicate says:
'acedia laughs when it sees a hermitage, it is ready to
defeat and settle down'. For this reason the Carthusian
monks and all solitaries must abhor acedia under all
conditions, they must reject it completely through a
sensible experience of time and a surrender to the
power of God ...

The devil of acedia causes all kinds of bad moods,
headaches, the weakening of muscles, pain, stress and
cramps. On the third hour it even causes tremors and
aversion. Especially the first, the third and the ninth
hour, but also other moments, are dangerous. Around
the ninth hour, the acedia will falter and keep quiet.
But once dinner is served, it arouses from its sleep ...
and settles down alive and well in the corporal senses
and needs. The moment of prayer after the siesta, the
body feels heavy. When the monk wakes for prayer,
acedia will continue in sleepiness, by opening the
mouth quite inappropriately – this means by yawning –
and it restrains the psalm version from the monk's lips.

Keep the following in mind: acedia will struggle when the monk stands up. It invites the monk to sit down and to cross his legs. It will tempt him to sit down on a chair or in a seat; however, it is much better to stand upright for God. Once you sit down, the acedia will encourage you to lean on the backrest, and because you sit down, it will encourage your whole back to lean to the backrest. And those who stand upright will be encouraged to bend a little bit more and to lean against the wall.[160]

The perseverance or persistence of the solitary monk

In an analogy with the ancient monastic tradition, the Carthusian writings resolve the problem of the acedia or spiritual apathy with the unequivocal answer of perseverance (*perseverantia*). Only one who remains faithful to the cell, and who is able to resist all temptations to escape, will be strong enough to control his thoughts and fantasies. Dom Jean-Baptiste Porion (d. 1987), once procurator of the Carthusian order in Rome, wrote: 'The feelings of fatigue, of physical exhaustion during the day and of apathy for all requirements of our lifestyle, are essential temptations of each Carthusian monk. It is the battle we have to fight because we entrusted our lives to God. We feel as though we have been thrown into an ocean. Patience is the only solution: we have to live a hidden life in communion with God each and every single day.'[161]

---

[160] Denys le Chartreux, *Commentaire de l'Echelle du Paradis*, in *Opera Omnia* 28, p. 221–5.

[161] J. B. Porion, *personal letters* (kept in the archives of the Grande Chartreuse), p. 53.

Also Dom Marcellin Theeuwes confirms the importance of time in monastic life. Especially during the first years, new monks must learn to be patient and to fight doubts and personal weaknesses: 'You must overcome all kind of obstacles. And the greatest obstacle of all is doubt. "I had serious doubts about my own possibilities. That was really hard to bear. I had no doubts about my vocation or about the Lord's presence and grace. But I had doubts about myself. Would I be capable? Would I be happy? I was twenty-four years old when I entered the Carthusian order. All kinds of doubts showed up. Sometimes I could not concentrate, or I felt the need to throw all my books out of the window. I often thought that I had the flu. But the doctor always said that I wasn't sick. It took two years, and suddenly all doubts disappeared. The sun broke through. I don't know why or when." In his first years as a monk, Dom Marcellin had a lot of doubts. But he learned to be patient and to yearn. But it takes time, that is for sure.'[162]

St Anthony says that the cell must have the same significance for a hermit as the water for the fish: 'Just as fish die if they stay too long out of water, so the monks who loiter outside their cells or pass their time with men of the world lose the intensity of inner peace. So, like a fish going towards the sea, we must hurry to reach our cell, for fear that if we delay outside we will lose our interior watchfulness.'[163] Also Guigo I was inspired by St Anthony's metaphor and he compared the solitary monk with a fish

[162] L. Feijen, *De reis van je hoofd naar je hart*, p. 132.
[163] Antonius, *Les Apophtegmes des Pères* I (SC 387), p. 124.

or a sheep who cannot live without water or a stable: 'The inhabitant of the cell must be alert, diligent and careful not to invent or allow any occasions to leave the cell, unless on the prescribed hours. The cell is as necessary for his salvation as the water is for the fish or the stable for the sheep. The longer he remains in the cell, the more he will be happy to live in it. But when he gets used to leaving the cell quite often and for all kinds of bagatelles, he will soon hate it. For this reason he may ask for everything he needs in the prescribed hours. And what is received must be kept with care.' The subject of perseverance as the ultimate answer to acedia is regularly repeated in the writings of the Carthusian tradition. We quote some fragments from the letters of Bernard from Portes and Denys the Carthusian:

> How to resist the temptations of the enemy? It is quite usual for a hermit to be confused by the temptations of the devil or to be afflicted by bouts of sadness. The enemy knows precisely how to approach God's servants and how to disturb them during prayers and spiritual activities. He tries to whisper sadness, or anger, injustice, pride, impure thoughts, disinterest or sleep. He tries to distract the spirit or to avoid the striving for holiness ... Arm yourself against all these emotions and temptations and against all nightly illusions.[164]
>
> A patient who leaves the infirmary without being healed risks being affected by an even worse disease. And the fugitive who leaves his prison will be arrested

---

[164] Bernard de Portes, *Lettre au reclus Raynaud*, pp. 69–70.

and executed. Your infirmary – sinner – is your cell.
You escaped to it when you left the world. So remain
in the cell with perseverance. When you do not, you
will lose outwardly everything that you have gained
inwardly. If you cannot control your body from
moving or wandering, you will be unable to direct your
spirit to one single goal. In the outside world there are
many things which impede a pure, spiritual and moral
life. When there is a good reason or occasion to leave
the cell, try to control your senses and to restrain your
tongue. Climacus[165] says that the soul must inculcate a
divine presence: the spirit will be able to restrain from
impure thoughts and wandering and the inhabitant of
the cell will be able to enter and leave as much as he
wants. There is only one thing that the devil enjoys in
solitary life: constant movement! Stability on the other
hand will be pleasing to God.[166]

For a beginner, who is not yet resistant and who
still has need for daily care, the cell is an infirmary,
a kind of pharmacy with medications like a hospital.
He must remain in the cell and patiently await the
visit of the doctor. He must be aware of every decline
which might damage and cause the concupiscences
of the world to enter by conversation or encounter
… The great Arsenius[167] once said: 'If you want to be
saved, escape from the world, keep silent and search

---

[165] St John Climacus: a famous monk who lived on Mount Sinai during the seventh
    century.
[166] Denys le Chartreux, *La vie et la fin du solitaire*, pp. 69–70.
[167] St Arsenius the Great (d. 445) is one of the Egyptian Desert Fathers.

for peace.' When the monks asked him why he didn't join community meetings or recreation, he answered them: 'Excuse me. God knows that I love you all. But I cannot be with God and men at the same time.' ... Another Desert Father says: 'Remain in your cell and your cell will be your teacher.' And St Anthony, the greatest among all hermits, says: 'Do not be too quick to leave the place where you arrived.' ...

For the heroic contemplative, the cell is a place of salvation, the essence of inner peace; the site of significant contemplation; a heavenly residence; a place of abundant comfort; an utter joy. St Anthony, the most eminent among all hermits, says rightly that the cell is as necessary for the monk as the water for the fish. A monk who wanders unnecessarily outside his cell will die, just like a fish on dry land. Someone once said very cleverly: a monk who remains unceasing in his cell is a source of many good things. The inhabitant of the cell who has had a taste of the inner encounter with God and the sweet fruits of solitary life will fear to leave his cell. And when it is necessary to do so, he will make a sign of the cross and pray, as though he leaves a fortress, a robust castle, a privileged place to hide from the enemy ... My brother, beware! The good custom is to remain in your cell from the beginning, with an inborn wisdom, like a bride in the bridal room. May the cell embrace you with tenderness. Observe its attractive beauty, remain in your cell and do not search for joy in other places.[168]

The liturgical tradition of the Carthusian order

The Carthusian liturgy: a proper heritage and rite

The Carthusian life is totally directed to the praise of God. For this reason the daily schedule is balanced with moments of solitary and common prayer, of manual labour and study, of wakefulness and sleep. The balance of all the different activities directs the monk's spirit towards inner union with God. It is his vocation, his goal and his only reason for existence: the *work* of the Carthusian monks is the *work of God*, the *opus Dei*. The whole spiritual cycle hinges on the succession of the liturgical offices. They define the structure and the rhythm of the monk's personal search for God and his intercession for the world and the Church. 'When celebrating the Divine Office, the monks are the voice and heart of the Church,' as we read in the statutes of the Carthusian order. 'Through them, the Church presents to the Father, in Christ, praise, supplication, adoration, and humble petition for pardon. The monk fulfils this important role by his whole existence, but in a more explicit and public way in the liturgy … Since our vocation is to remain ever awake to the presence of God, our whole life becomes a liturgy, whether we offer the official prayer of the Church, or follow the movement of our heart. This liturgy becomes

---

[168] Denys le Chartreux, *Eloge de la vie en solitude*, pp. 215–17.

more explicit at times; but the diversity is by no means a source of division, since it is always the same Lord who exercises his priesthood in us, praying to the Father in the one Spirit.'[169]

In the spirit of the Second Vatican Council, the statutes define the liturgy as the culmination and source of the life of the Church:

> We who have left everything to seek God alone and to possess him more fully, should carry out the liturgical functions with particular reverence. For when we accomplish the liturgy, especially the eucharistic celebration, we have access to the Father through his Son, the Word Incarnate, who suffered and was glorified in the outpouring of the Holy Spirit … When we celebrate the divine worship in choir, or recite the office in the cell, it is the prayer of the Church which is being offered by our lips; for the prayer of Christ is one, and through the sacred liturgy, this one prayer is wholly present in each member. Among solitary monks, liturgical acts are manifest in a special way. In the nature of the Church humanity is directed and subjected to the divine, the visible to the invisible, action to contemplation … Thus, through the sacred rites, we are able to express the deeper aspirations of the Spirit, and prayer, springing from the depths of the heart. When it finds an echo in the sacred words of the liturgy, it acquires a new perfection. Again,

---

[169]   Statutes of the Carthusian order, 3.21.

communal prayer, which we make our own through the liturgical action, is carried over into solitary prayer through which we offer to God an intimate sacrifice of praise, transcending all words. For the solitude of the cell is the place where a soul, enamoured of silence, and forgetful of human cares, shares in the fullness of the mystery by which Christ crucified, rising from the dead, returns to the bosom of the Father. A monk, therefore, provided he strives continually to cling to God, exemplifies within himself what is signified by the entire liturgy.[170]

St Bruno and the first Carthusians returned radically to original monastic simplicity, because it adapted better to their ascetic and solitary lifestyle and the small community of hermits. Liturgy needed to be simple and moderate. It had to direct the monk's spirit towards union with God. Bruno and his companions constructed a proper liturgical heritage, inspired by the Western doctor of the Church Peter Damiani (d. 1072) and the Camaldolese monks of Fonte Avellana in Tuscany. Some liturgical elements are literally borrowed from the Camaldolese tradition, for example the public confession in chapter. Other inspirations come from the Caroling liturgy of the canons of St-Rufus in Avignon, where two of Bruno's first disciples belonged, for example some rituals for the dead. The proper missal of the Carthusian order also contains elements from the local rites and the liturgical books of Grenoble, Valence

---

[170]   Statutes of the Carthusian order, 6.41.

and Vienne. According to the opinion of the historian and Carthusian monk Augustin Devaux, the author of a very detailed study on the genesis of the Carthusian missal,[171] Bruno and his first companions had no other choice than to invent a proper *liturgical consensus* because of their different backgrounds and customs. Bruno himself was influenced by his past in the chapter of Reims and in the abbey of Molesmes, likewise his disciples by the liturgical inheritances of their own origins.

However, the first Carthusian community simplified, transformed and adapted each inspired or borrowed liturgical practice from other traditions according to the standards of a solitary life in the desert. All additional prayers, hymns and songs were abolished and replaced by long moments of silence. Processions were excluded, as well as solemn liturgical vestments, incense, golden or silver vessels (except the chalice), ornaments in the church and the use of organs or musical instruments. Moreover, Guigo I shortened all antiphons and conserved only the simplest melodies to avoid multiple rehearsals. Dom Augustin Devaux concludes that the compilation of the proper antiphonary of the Carthusian order is based on three principles: the omission of all non-biblical texts, the shortening of the entire liturgical repertoire to safeguard a spirit of simplicity and a prohibition on composing new melodies. Some of these liturgical restrictions are written down in *The Customs*

---

[171]   Cf. A. Devaux, *Les origines du missel des chartreux* (AC 99: 32), pp. 1–107; H. J. Becker, 'Die Responsorien des Kartäuserbreviers' (doctoral thesis), Theological Faculty, Munich, 1971.

of Chartreuse: 'It is important to notice that we never keep processions for whatever solemnity and that feasts or vigils are never transferred ... Each Sunday after the office of None we gather in the cloister for a rehearsal of the songs and to make other necessary arrangements. Because we preserve silence in the cells during the whole week, we confess this day our sins to the Prior or to someone who is charged with this task ... We have no golden or silver ornaments in the church, except for the chalice and the little pipe to consume the Blood of the Lord.[172] We have no wall decorations, no tapestries.'[173]

The rhythm of the liturgical year consists of the alternation of ordinary and seasonal times: the cycle of Advent, Christmastide, Lent and the Easter season. The Divine Offices during the ordinary time may be of a triple kind in the Carthusian liturgy: the office of Sundays, the office of solemnities and feasts, where there may be a difference between great solemnities with candles and common feasts without candles, and the office of the saints. The office of the saints may be of a fourfold kind: a solemnity or feast with candles, a common feast with twelve lectures, a feast with three lectures and a common memory. The rhythm of the Carthusian life is defined by the rhythm of the liturgical year and the natural seasons. Each liturgical time corresponds with the proper colour of a certain season and therefore with a certain spiritual mood. 'During Christmastide, the psalms contain a distinct

---

[172]   The first Carthusians consumed the wine in the chalice with a small pipe or straw.
[173]   *Customs of Chartreuse*, 6, 1; 7, 1–2; 40, 1.

significance and warmth. The liturgy sings and invites us to sing'[174] – a Carthusian monk witnesses to his personal experience of Christmas. Lent and winter on the other hand evoke a completely different spiritual mood:

> The liturgy is dressed in sombre clothes and stripped of all Alleluias and Glorias. It invites us to reduce life itself and to reject all abundances. Lent is a period of secret and latent germination, always enlightened by hope and expectation. The liturgy invites us to repentance and renewal of life, in Christ. It encourages us to recognise our true face through authenticity and keenness of thought, through prayer and love, in order to be prepared for a more intense experience of reality according to the example of Christ. The mystery of Christ is present in our own being: it is who we are and who we should become. His suffering is ours. Our cross is his cross, carried by his love. Our true life is the resurrection of Christ. The liturgy puts us in the footsteps of Christ: it teaches us that his way is ours also. The dramatic commemoration is more than the commemoration of an historic event. It is the experience of the sufferings of Christ, here and now, for us! We must make a choice for faith and love. Christ survived the struggle with sin and death. Through the sacramental celebration of the mystery of the Passion we share in the glorious power of his life and his love. Through the Eucharistic sacrifice and

---

[174]   Un Chartreux, *Vivre dans l'intimité du Christ* (2005/1), p. 84.

the other sacraments, the Word of Christ is effected in the declaration of the Church (the Church is the Word of God) and through the symbols, gestures and words of the Church. This is true for the entire liturgical cycle ... it is the fundamental strength which makes us one with Christ in his Body, the Church.[175]

From the beginning the Carthusian monks sang the liturgy in Gregorian chant; however, in some monasteries Divine Office and Mass are celebrated in the local language. With the spread of Gregorian chant, Pope Gregory the Great (540–604) intended a unity in the liturgy in the entire Western Church. Nevertheless, this process could not prevent the survival or even the rise of local and regional liturgical traditions, for example the Ambrosian rite in Milan or the Mozarabic rite in Toledo and Zaragosa (Spain). The Carthusian liturgy is such a particular tradition, preserved uninterrupted and integral to the present day. The separation from the outside world and the privacy of the Carthusian communities contributed to the survival of this proper patrimony. So the Carthusian monks still sing the intact liturgical cycle from the eleventh century, admittedly with some small changes and adaptions here and there.

The Gregorian melodies of the Carthusian tradition are quite different from the original Roman Gregorian chant, especially that which emerged from the tradition of the Benedictine abbey of Solesmes. It has already been noted that the Carthusians tried to avoid multiple rehearsals to

---

[175]   Un Chartreux, *Vivre dans l'intimité du Christ*, pp. 110–11.

protect the solitude of the monks. That is why all non-biblical texts and difficult melodies were abrogated and replaced by long periods of silence. The Carthusian Ordinary of the Mass contains merely three Kyries, two Glorias and one Credo, and all Alleluias have been shortened or removed. The sombre melodies without organ or instruments and the slow pace of the songs reflect the spiritual pillars of simplicity and repentance of the Carthusian order. The slow pace of the doxology *Gloria Patri et Filio et Spiritui Sancto* at the end of each psalm is a typical example. Those who wish to taste the Carthusian Gregorian chant, may listen to one of the CDs recorded in the monasteries of Serra San Bruno, Parkminster or the Grande Chartreuse.[176]

The Divine Office (in community as well as in solitude) is considered a participation in the prayer of the universal Church and a realisation of the sanctification of all humanity. The monks must pray the different offices with attention, devotion and discipline. The statutes insist on attention to the proper significance of the liturgical texts and songs, especially the importance of the psalms. The monk must keep his attention during prayer and must sing harmoniously with the others. 'Let us observe this manner of chanting, singing in the sight of the most Holy Trinity and the holy angels, penetrated with fear of God and aflame with a deep desire. May the songs we sing raise our minds to the contemplation of eternal realities, and our voices

---

[176]   Here are some references to a few CDs with the original Carthusian melodies: *Hosanna. Ufficio della note delle Palme. Canti dei Monaci della Certosa di Serra San Bruno; Spes Mea. Canti Gregoriani. Ufficio e Messa di San Bruno secondo il rito Certosino; In the Silence of the Word. A Carthusian Plainchant Meditation by the Monks of Parkminster.*

blend into one cry of jubilation before God our Creator.'[177] In the sixteenth century, Dom Joannes-Justus Lanspergius (d. 1539), a Carthusian monk from Cologne, noted the following encouragement in one of his letters: 'Wake up immediately when the bell rings and do not stay in your bed, as one negligence of this kind gives birth to ten others. Do not spare your voice during the Divine Office, but use this talent given by God with joy. Do not try to imitate the chant of the others, but try to memorise the songs, or use a book if you feel unsure. Superficiality sings and gazes here and there. Nonchalance and every infraction against discipline must be dispelled immediately. Attune your voice to the voice of the cantor and avoid acceleration or abbreviation of the divine hymns.'[178]

Those who have the opportunity to assist at the Divine Office in a Carthusian community will notice how simply and authentically it is accomplished. In the Grande Chartreuse, the visitors may follow the office from a balcony at the rear of the church. From this high 'swallow's nest' one can observe the monks who enter the church one by one, bending with respect for the altar, passing the rope to one another to ring the bell and taking their place in choir. With a modest tap, the prior marks the beginning of the service. After a short moment of silent prayer, the psalmody resounds into the domes. With two or three monks, the texts and staves are followed in very ancient and large books. Just as simply as the office begins, so it comes to an end. Without a single

---

[177] Statutes of the Carthusian order, 7.52.
[178] J.-J. Lanspergius, *Epistolae paraeneticae ac morales, Opera Omnia,* Letter XII, pp. 113–17.

word or sign, the white monks disappear into their solitary
and silent cells. In the Carthusian monasteries of Serra San
Bruno and Portes we were invited to join the community in
choir, as well as to concelebrate during Mass. Even in the
sacristy, the same spirit of simplicity and silence reigns. It
may look a little bit strange to outsiders, but every gesture
or movement during the liturgy has a proper sense for the
Carthusian monks: they are sacred acts accomplished only
for God.

The Carthusian Matins: *the office at midnight*

Each night around 11.30 p.m. the Carthusian monks wake
up for Matins and Lauds at midnight. They have chosen a
life of constant vigilance, like the ten wise virgins who took
their lamps and went out to meet the bridegroom (cf. Matt.
25:1–13). As the Prior of Serra San Bruno preached during
a profession service:

> We watch the sky because we await the return of the
> Son of Man. A Carthusian monk receives a very unique
> mission: to wait for the Lord and to receive Him once
> He appears. We do not know when He will return, but
> it is sure that He will return from the wedding soon.
> We are joyful, because we are ready to open as soon
> as He knocks. We must be willing and attentive, awake
> constantly. To stay awake is a most typical quality of
> the Carthusian monk. It is night, because Jesus, who is
> the Light, left us. But we may not sleep or rest. We must
> wake in silence. Even more importantly we must not
> lose our attention through dreaming, or other types of
> attractive ideas, or by absence. A Carthusian monk has

nothing else to do other than keep his eyes open and his heart vigilant. The Carthusian apostolate consists in being wholly awake for the return of the Lord. It is not our vocation to give advice or to preach. By showing the world the direction humanity must face and by advancing the coming of the Kingdom of God through prayer, we receive our only raison d'être.[179]

Carthusian monks interrupt their sleep as a living sign of this biblical vigilance for the return of Christ. Around midnight, the entire community gathers in the church for the offices of Matins and Lauds. Before night prayer, each monk prays the Matins of Our Lady in his cell. According to the liturgical season, night prayer can take two or even three hours. This interrupted sleep is quite unique in Western monasticism, because almost no other order or congregation still holds this practice, not even the Camaldolese, the Trappists or the Monastic Family of Bethlehem.[180] The custom of night watch comes from the Desert Fathers and the early Christian communities of hermits. Dom Marcellin Theeuwes tells about the significance of night prayer:

> In the Bible as well as in the experience of men, night is an excellent time for prayer and encounter with God. Anchorites rise at night, because the night watch is 'a holy and persistent wakefulness for the return of the Lord', as written in the statutes of the order.

---

[179]   Un Certosino, *Ferventi d'amore divino*, p. 85.
[180]   There are still a few Benedictine abbeys who hold (or have restored) the practice of night prayer, for example in France.

Around midnight, the bell calls for prayer. So we wake to praise the wonders of God and to receive his Word. Silence and darkness support this experience. We have nothing else to do other than be sensitive to the presence of God. Night watch is a time for being alone with God. When we wake in the morning, we do not have the same experience. From the moment I awake, my spirit is occupied with all kinds of activities: a service for one of the monks, a task which needs to be accomplished, etc. But during the night, only God is present! The night office is quite long, two or three hours, for solemnities it is even longer. The psalmody nourishes inner contemplation and the prayer of the heart. We are able to surrender peacefully to the Word of God who speaks in the intimate silence of our heart, without any fatigue or effort.[181]

Night prayer is a means of physical asceticism, because the biological human rhythm is radically interrupted. Each night, the Carthusian monk has to awake from his sleep and leave his warm bed. As he is not a nocturnal animal, he has to confront darkness and cold. It is an extreme effort, especially during the long, snowy winters. It may take a long time to adapt physically to the interruption of sleep. The human body may never get accustomed to it. The Carthusian monks try to go to bed and to fall asleep as quickly as possible, to resume their sleep after the night office. This practice may seem inhuman to outsiders, but for the monks night

---

[181] S. Pruvot, *Entretien avec Dom Marcellin*, p. 13.

prayer occurs at the most intimate moments of the day. The former Carthusian Kris Wittevrongel agrees: 'If there is one thing I miss, it is certainly night prayer. I remember some very intense and beautiful moments. The dark church with only a few lamps to read, the songs with one accord during the night render a very soothing atmosphere. For me it was never hard to interrupt my sleep, because you can sleep seven or eight hours a day. Still five years later, I awake after four hours of sleep.'[182] Even Denys the Carthusian affirms the privileged moment of encounter with God during night prayer:

> The Lord teaches us to seek first the kingdom and his righteousness (cf. Matt. 6:33). That is why we have to start the day with divine worship, especially with prayer, praise and thanks. A small mistake in the beginning always becomes bigger. We must begin, accomplish and end night office with great devotion, purity and zeal. After sufficient sleep, which is often fulfilled with deep and pure meditations and even with divine revelations, the hermit and each monk who is worthy to be called by this name must awaken and begin the day with the Our Father and the Hail Mary, or with the antiphon 'Come Holy Spirit', or with this joyful version: 'Come Creator Spirit, penetrate our thoughts and fulfil the hearts you have made with mercy.' ... We have to rise with joy and devotion for night prayer and we must awake from our sleepiness. Waiting for

---

[182]   J. Vranckx, *Ik was een kartuizer*, p. 5.

the sign of our King (the knocking of the host), we must behave as the guests at the wedding banquet, by emerging from the place of misery, that is our bed, which is a real image of the grave on which we sleep as dead men. Let us joyfully sing the hymns of the Lord. The cold night may not frighten us, nor discourage all efforts. Our lips must shout for joy when psalms are sung for the Creator (cf. Ps. 71:23). While it is still dark outside, our inner light must burn. The night is a privileged moment, because sorrows or noise do not disturb. The night helps us to raise the soul to the Lord and to sing and pray vivaciously. The external senses are less influenced during the night and even imagination is less strong.[183]

Nourished by the Bread: the Eucharist in the Carthusian order

'The Church draws her life from the Eucharist,' writes Pope John Paul II in his encyclical letter *Ecclesia de Eucharistia* (2003). In line with the tradition of the Church, the Carthusian order understands the daily celebration of Mass as the summit or highpoint of the personal encounter with God. 'When we assemble for the Eucharist, the unity of the Carthusian family is consummated in Christ, who is himself present, and at prayer.'[184] This is written in the statutes of the order. Nevertheless to safeguard the solitude of the monks, Mass was only celebrated on Sundays and obligatory feasts (around 236 times a year) in the early days of the Carthusian

---

[183] Denys le Chartreux, *Eloge de la vie en solitude*, pp. 178–81.
[184] Statutes of the Carthusian order, 3.21.

order. During the Middle Ages it was not common to receive holy communion each day, so the *spiritual communion* was a widespread custom in Western Europe. Only in 1222 was the daily celebration of the Eucharist introduced in the Carthusian order. For this reason Guigo I prescribes in *The Customs of Chartreuse,* 'Mass is seldom sung here, because silence and solitude in the cell are our principal intention and concern.'[185] Until the middle of the sixteenth century, the Carthusians practised the so-called *missa ficta* or the *nudum officium*: when a feast coincided with a Sunday or a vigil (the eve of a feast), priority was rendered to the Eucharist of that particular Sunday or vigil. As compensation the lections of the feast were read in a kind of Mass without a consecration prayer and without bread or wine. Until the seventeenth century, the Carthusian novices and the non-ordained monks only received communion on Sunday and once during the week, unless the prior allowed them to take communion more frequently.

Nowadays, the Carthusian monks celebrate the sacrament of the Eucharist twice a day. The entire community participates at the Convent Mass, which is celebrated by one of the priests in the morning. During the day, quite often after the Convent Mass or after Vespers, each priest celebrates also a private Mass in solitude. That is why each Carthusian monastery contains different chapels and altars. Only the Carthusian and the Jesuit order received a Roman indult to celebrate Mass without the participation of the

---

[185]   *Customs of Chartreuse*, 14.5.

faithful.[186] 'The commemoration of the Lord's sacrifice brings together every day all the cloister monks, as well as the lay monks who so desire. In addition, the monks who are priests celebrate a Eucharist in solitude, united with the entire Church. Then, the humble offering of their life in the desert is taken up into that of Christ, for the glory of God the Father. On days when the community aspect of our life is more in evidence, the monks may concelebrate, united in one priesthood.'[187]

The particular eucharistic rite and the particular missal of the Carthusian order contain some remarkable customs and rituals which are different from the Roman rite and other monastic traditions. The principal celebrant of the Convent Mass or the lonely celebrant of the private Mass prostrates on the steps of the altar before the celebration begins. Only after this quite long moment of silent prayer does the priest put on the liturgical vestments in the sacristy. The priest venerates the altar with a kiss and makes a sign of the cross in silence, while he crosses the index and the ring finger and the thumb of his right hand as a confession of the trinitarian unity of God, just as is the custom of the Eastern Orthodox traditions. The wine is put in the chalice before the celebration of the Eucharist begins, while water is only added at the moment of the offertory, followed by the hand-washing.

---

[186] Cf. canon 906 in the Code of Canon Law: 'Except for a just and reasonable cause, a priest is not to celebrate the eucharistic sacrifice without the participation of at least some member of the faithful.'

[187] Statutes of the Carthusian order, 3.21.

Convent Mass is always assisted by a deacon or an acolyte. The deacon reads the Gospel and the acolyte serves the altar. They have their place in the choir among the other monks. The Eucharistic Prayer is prayed in total silence. The priest stretches his arms widely in the form of a cross. Only the Bread is elevated during the consecration, while the monks prostrate in the stalls and the bell is sounded in the tower. When Mass is concelebrated with several priests, the Eucharistic Prayer is prayed quite often in the local language or in Latin. The entire community gathers around the altar before the sign of peace and the Agnus Dei. The celebration of the Eucharist ends with the conclusion prayer, but without a blessing.

In one of his meditations, Guigo II speaks about the intrinsic connection between the mystery of the Eucharist and solitary contemplation in the cell: 'When our spirit rises unto the clouds, we may meet many known as well as unknown realities. If we understand the way our body eats and drinks, than we may understand how the spirit eats and drinks in his own way. If we eat real bread for example, we put first a little piece in our mouth, we crack it with our teeth, we make it liquid with our drool and we swallow it so that the nutrients strengthen the body. Well, the spiritual bread is Christ. He is the living Bread descended from heaven for the nourishment of his people. We receive this bread through faith and contemplation in the life to come. Through faith Christ lives in us, and faith in Christ is Christ in our hearts. The more strongly we believe in Christ, the more strongly we receive Him.'[188]

Nourished by the Word: *lectio divina* in the Carthusian order

According to Dom Marcellin Theeuwes, the rediscovery of the Scriptures is one of the greatest gifts for the Church during the past decades. *Lectio divina*, or the spiritual reading of the Bible, is

> no theological or exegetic approach to the text, but rather a meditative reading in order to give one's own personal existence an enlightened understanding about God, salvation, inner repentance and a conversion towards the Spirit. In the lasting contact with the sacred text, the divine and Christian significance of human existence and reality will slowly appear. One discovers how God really desires to meet his people. The biblical revelation becomes a personal revelation. God acts in the same way with all who are called by Him and at the same time He acts quite personally with each of them. The sense which is given to history in the Scriptures is also the sense of our personal life … In this spirit, the reading of the Bible received a central place in the life of the ancient monks under the magnificent name *lectio divina*. A divine reading not only of the sacred text, but through the text of your own person and life.

---

[188]   Guiges II le Chartreux, *Lettre sur la vie contemplative*, p. 180.

> The Spirit who inspired the sacred text transforms the Word of the Scripture into a personal Word in our heart. For this reason, the reading of the Bible was no secondary occupation for the ancient monks, but it unites with silent prayer as the two sides of a coin or as the same movement up and down: God and humanity, who search for each other and who speak with each other from heart to heart.[189]

The statutes of the order prescribe that 'the monk unceasingly meditates on the Holy Scriptures, until they become part of him'.[190]

Carthusian literature often refers to Psalm 34 to explain the significance of the spiritual reading: 'Oh, taste and see that the LORD is good; happy are those who take refuge in him' (Ps. 34:8). The Word of God – that 'is very near to you, it is in your mouth and in your heart for you to observe' (cf. Deut. 30:14) – must be chewed over and over again so that it penetrates the human spirit entirely. In the footsteps of famous monastic authors Origin, John Cassian and Benedict, the Carthusian writers like to refer to the version of 'the eating of the Word' in the Apocalypse of St John to speak about *lectio divina*: 'So I went to the angel and told him to give me the little scroll; and he said to me, 'Take it, and eat; it will be bitter to your stomach, but sweet as honey in your mouth' (Rev. 10:9). That is why 'the prior should willingly provide his monks with books, since these are

---

[189]   M. Theeuwes, *Bruno van Keulen* ..., pp. 110–11.

[190]   Statutes of the Carthusian order, 3.21.

the imperishable food of the soul. It is fitting that monks should find their nourishment primarily in Holy Scripture, the Fathers of the Church, and proven monastic authors. He is to supply them also with other books of sound quality, carefully selected for their usefulness to each individual. For in solitude we read not to be informed about the latest opinions but so that faith may be nourished in peace and prayer may be fostered.'[191]

The ladder of monks': four rungs towards God's Word

Guigo II regarded *lectio divina* as a means to reach divine wisdom. Drop by drop, the monk absorbs the divine truth through the meditation of Holy Scripture. Meditation unifies the Word and the soul. In his *Letter on Contemplative Life*, Guigo II devises the idea of the so-called *scala claustralium* or the 'ladder of monks'. By four rungs of repentance, one is able to ascend towards God: lecture, meditation, prayer and contemplation. Later authors reduced the ladder to the first three steps, because the gift of contemplation is quite rare. Reading, meditating and praying are an indivisible triumvirate in Carthusian spirituality. Guigo II writes as follows:

> When I was hard at work one day, thinking on the spiritual work necessary for God's servants, four such spiritual works came to my mind, these being: reading, meditation, prayer and contemplation. This is the monks' ladder by which they can climb from earth to

---

[191] Statutes of the Carthusian order, 3.23.

heaven. It is a marvellously tall ladder, but with just four rungs, the one end standing on the ground, the other thrilling into the clouds and showing the climber heavenly secrets ... Understand now what the four rungs of this ladder are, each in turn. Reading is busily looking on Holy Scripture with all one's will and wit. Meditation is a studious searching with the mind to know what was hitherto concealed through want of proper skill. Prayer is a devout desiring of the heart to gain what is good and avoid what is evil. Contemplation is the lifting up of the heart to God, tasting something of the heavenly sweetness and savour. Reading seeks, meditation finds, prayer asks, contemplation feels ... The first degree is for beginners, the second for those profiting from it, the third for those who are devout, the fourth for those who are holy and blessed of God.[192]

The first step is the *level of the lips*: the monk has to whisper the text while he reads it. *The Customs of Chartreuse* establish an explicit moment for *lectio divina* during the day: 'the time between lunch and the None is reserved for reading or other spiritual exercises.'[193] For Guigo II, spiritual reading was like food which the spirit must swallow and absorb through meditation. With the image of the grapes, he illustrates how the Word of God is understood by the spirit and absorbed by the heart, in the way that teeth must chew

---

[192] Guiges II le Chartreux, *Lettre sur la vie contemplative*, pp. 83–5.
[193] *Customs of Chartreuse*, 7, 8.

carefully on the seeds to taste the flavour. The external Word of God penetrates the inner spirit. Through the act of reading, the Word is peeled so that only the soft pulp reaches the act of meditation. The act of reading creates a comfortable relationship between the reader and the text. One's heart becomes porous for the significance of the text and transforms one's lifestyle into the act of imitation.

'Reading puts as it were whole food into our mouth; meditation chews it and breaks it down; prayer finds its taste and flavour; contemplation is the sweetness that so delights and strengthens us. Reading is like the bark, the shell; meditation like the pith, the nut; prayer is in the desiring and asking; and contemplation is in the delight of the experience of sweetness. Reading is the first ground that precedes and leads one into meditation; meditation seeks busily, and also with deep thought digs and delves deeply to find the treasure; and because it cannot be attained by itself alone, we are led into prayer that is mighty and strong.'[194]

The act of meditation comes after the act of reading: it invites the monk into the act of praying. For Guigo II, meditation was no intellectual or theoretical exegesis, but a sensitive experience of the deeper significance of the text. This is quite obvious from the use of metaphors like 'digging' and 'chewing' to illustrate the act of meditating. Meditation is above all a movement of descending: in the intimate room of our heart, we become familiar with the significance of the Word. The next movement is a movement of ascending: the imitation of the written message within our personal

---

[194]   Guiges II le Chartreux, *Lettre sur la vie contemplative*, pp. 85–7.

lifestyle. Without the fruits, meditation remains infertile, as we read repeatedly in the Carthusian literature.

Prayer is for Guigo II the desire for God or even the tasting of God. Spiritual reading, meditation and solitude will help the monk to reach the act of prayer. Prayer is an expression of pure love. The Carthusian authors use words like *amor* (love), *affectio* (affection), *delectare* (to give pleasure), *desiderare* (to desire) and even *sponsa* and *sponsus* (bride and groom). The act of praying brings the acts of reading and meditating to life in an extremely personal way. Guigo II writes: 'Lord, I have sought and thought with all my poor heart; and, Lord, in my meditation the fire of desire kindles to know you, not only the bitter bark without, in feeling and tasting in my soul ... But as much, Lord, as the puppy eats of the crumbs that fall from the table of the Lord, I ask of the heritage that is to come one drop of the heavenly joy to comfort my thirsty soul that burns in love-longing for you.'[195]

The act of contemplation at last is the final goal in spiritual reading: the acts of reading and meditating focus on the written words in the text, the act of praying and above all the act of contemplating make real a silent union between the soul and the Word. The soul is fertilised and conceived by the Word: 'With these and other such desires the heart is enflamed ... What does God want – the One whose help is always with the righteous and who is even attentive to our prayer? God does not wait until the prayer is ended, but he breaks into the midst of the burning desire of that

---

[195]   Guiges II le Chartreux, *Lettre sur la vie contemplative*, p. 95.

thirsty soul, and with a secret balm of heavenly sweetness softens the soul and comforts it, and makes it so overcome with delight and joy that it forgets all earthly things for that hour, and he makes that soul lose itself in wonder, as if it were dead to its earthly self. And as in corporal works we are so overcome that we lose the guidance of reason, so in the ladder of contemplation our bodily stirrings are so cancelled out that the flesh does not win over the spirit but becomes one with the Spirit.'[196]

About one century later on, Guigo's namesake Guigo du Pont (d. 1297), himself a Carthusian monk of the Grande Chartreuse, worked out his interpretations about spiritual reading in his *Tractate on Contemplation*. He emphasised the art of listening, which is in the first place the art of keeping quiet. Only without speaking can one listen to what God is saying through God's Word. The saint, Desert Father and deacon Arsène (d. 450) once said, *'Fuge, tace, quiesce'* ('Flee, be silent and pray'). About *lectio divina*, Guigo du Pont writes: 'Certainly, a loving soul will find comfort with God through fervent spiritual reading. The soul desires knowledge. It wants to discern what pleases God and what does not. It wants to know God's commands and it wants to accomplish them. She does not desire wisdom in the eyes of others, but rather desires to receive God's grace by tasting the Scriptures. A loving soul will find divine rest trough a fervent and attentive meditation. The soul meditates by repenting regularly of its sins and faults; by praising the divine blessings received; by praising with love the holy life

---

[196]   Guiges II le Chartreux, *Lettre sur la vie contemplative*, p. 97.

of Christ in all its aspects and living according to its own capacities, and constantly desiring the heavenly promises.'[197]

Formation in the Carthusian order: the way from postulant to monk

'Nothing for softies or dreamers', says Kris Wittevrongel about Carthusian life, 'that is why eight or ten candidates leave the monastery after a while'.[198] The road from a postulant to a professed monk is long, hard and extremely confronting because of its radicalism. 'Many are called, but few are chosen' (Matt. 22:14). Above all, the Carthusian life is a personal answer to a vocation. But the authenticity of the vocation has to be discerned accurately. Is the response to this vocation really sincere or are there other motives? Is it a well-considered and a balanced choice? The Carthusian life does not merely require a strong body but even more a stable, adult and equable mind. Dom Marcellin Theeuwes reminds us of the enormous gap between the ancient monastic tradition and the milieu of potential candidates:

> The young among us did not grow up in the same cultural and religious environment as the older monks and they are often shaped by the culture of our society. They are more doubtful and their spiritual fundamentals are less strong and durable. It is not surprising that it is quite difficult for them to adapt to the Carthusian

[197] Guiges Du Pont, *De contemplatione* (AC 72:2), pp. 269, 271.
[198] J. Vranckx, *Ik was een kartuizer*, p. 5.

lifestyle and our religious and intellectual context. It is especially hard for them to engage for a whole lifetime. Many candidates knock on our door after a sudden and intense conversion at the age of 20 or 25 … We want to discover if the postulant is truly able to surrender to something that goes beyond reality. Is he really willing to be instructed and to receive teachings from others? What counts is the truth about God and about one's own self. He must accept and integrate his shortcomings … The main question remains his motivation. Is it strong enough, is it purified and religiously motivated to survive a whole lifetime? He will discover the answers bit by bit, for himself and for others.[199]

Those who think they may have a vocation to the Carthusian life must write a letter to the prior or prioress of the monastery which they desire to enter. There will be enquiry about the family, about past life and education, as well as the physical and psychological health of the candidate. It may be that a physician, a psychologist or even a psychiatrist might be consulted. Candidates may enter between the age of 20 and 45, unless the prior general and his council make a dispensation. They must be free of canonical impediments, marriage or perpetual vows in another religious institute. When the prior and the majority of the community agree that a candidate is fit, he will be invited for a retreat. A basic knowledge of Latin is desirable, or at least the intellectual

---

[199]   P. Drijvers, *De weg naar het wezenlijke*, pp. 116–17.

capacity to learn this is especially important for those who wish to become a monk of the choir or a priest.

The postulate: a time of discernment

Entrance into a Carthusian monastery begins with a postulate which may take three months or even a year. The postulant receives a hermitage and participates in all activities and offices. In the church and chapter he wears a black cape on top of his clothes. All his personal effects and money are carefully kept in a depot. It costs no money to enter, even when the candidate leaves after a few days or weeks.

The novitiate: a time of instruction

The postulant is received as a novice after the democratic vote of the entire community. The novitiate is mostly two years, but the prior may decide to extend this period. Some ancient rituals symbolise the formal entrance into the Carthusian order. The new novice receives a white habit and a black cape. As a sign of total surrender, he prostrates in the chapter hall and lays his hands in the prior's hands. After the sign of peace, the entire community accompanies the new novice to his cell. New converses are accompanied to the church as the symbolic start of a life of prayer and contemplation.

The novice master is in charge of the formation of all novices. He visits them regularly in their cells and instructs them in the history, statutes, liturgy and customs of the Carthusian order. The novice master is a kind of spiritual father who introduces the novices to the art of praying, the most important learning for a new monk. With a spirit of patience and wisdom, he tries to discern whether the candidate is really called to the solitary and ascetic lifestyle and whether he is physically and psychologically suited to it.

During the second year, the novice starts the cycle of philosophy and theology which prepares him for the priesthood. External professors or specialists are invited to the monastery for classes and conferences about exegesis, dogmatic theology, ethics and church history. If there are several novices, the lessons are organised together, otherwise held privately in the cell. Examinations, a thesis and the presentation of papers are an essential part of intellectual formation. Concerning the role of the novice master, an anonymous Carthusian monk once wrote:

> The formation of the novices is entrusted to the novice master. He is responsible for the monastic formation in the spirit of the Carthusian order, as well as for the moral and spiritual formation and advice in moments of affliction. He must awaken in them the love for Christ and the Church by modelling a deep spirit of prayer and intimate union with God. He must teach the novices how to use their freedom, their sacred freedom within our solitary vocation, as the statutes prescribe. His authority must focus on the freedom of the novices, because the only goal of formation is permanent engagement in the love of God. The formation is a love affair and a personal and reciprocal relationship. Without real freedom and spontaneity, it makes no sense. The companionship of the novice master must help the novice to discern the right path and the will of the Holy Spirit. The role of the novice

master is that of a servant ... Many qualities are required for this duty: discernment, maturity, charity, responsibility, love for his vocation, a contemplative and calm spirit, openness, agility, understanding, the heart of a mother and the authority of a father. That is all ...

I only ask one thing: when you read about all the qualities required by the statutes and the superiors, do not be afraid if the novice masters does not possess them all. The statutes have an ideal in mind, but the superiors realise the ideal according to their own capacities. One may have one strength, someone else another. We all have limitations. The only thing we may ask from the superiors is that their authority rests in the humble, singular effort to realise the ideal. Do not judge from outside. Maybe you, too, will be called to serve your brothers and you will have strengths and limitations. We are humans. Let us accept one another as humans. Be helpful to the superiors through wise co-operation. Remember that Christ acts in them and that He is able to write straight on crooked lines.[200]

Profession: the time of devotion

When the novice is accepted by the entire community, he may take his vows for a period of three years, the so-called *simple profession* in Carthusian parlance. These temporary vows may be renewed twice before the *solemn vows* follow after at least seven years of preparation. The studies for the

---

[200] Un Chartreux, *Vivre dans l'intimité du Christ* (2006/2), pp. 93–5.

priesthood continue. The candidate reads his handwritten profession formula before all his fellow brothers. After the words 'I promise' he writes the period of engagement or 'for ever' when he takes his solemn vows. The profession formula is almost identical to the Benedictine profession formula: 'I, Brother N., promise stability, obedience, and conversion of my life, before God, his saints, and the relics belonging to this hermitage, which was built in honour of God, the Blessed Mary ever Virgin, and St John the Baptist, in the presence of Dom N., Prior.'[201]

The converse novices must make a choice for a life as a donate or a lay brother. According to their choice, they take the *small donation* or the *small profession* for a period of three years and afterwards for a period of two years. Also the converses are instructed in the methods of prayer, in the spirituality, rituals and customs of the Carthusian order; however, the formation is less intellectual and theoretical. The formula of the donation is as follows: 'I, Brother N., for the love of our Lord Jesus Christ and for the salvation of my soul, promise to serve God faithfully as a donate for the building up of the Church, observing obedience and chastity, and living without personal possessions. I therefore give myself to this house in a mutually binding contract, to serve it at all times, and submit myself to the discipline of the order, according to the statutes.'[202]

A solemnly professed monk or converse is considered to be a member of the order and of a certain monastery.

---

[201]   Statutes of the Carthusian order, 1.10.

[202]   Statutes of the Carthusian order, 1.19.

He wears the typical Carthusian habit. Just before he pronounces his vows, he kneels before each monk and begs, 'Brother, pray for me.' The parchment profession formula is read and placed on the altar. When the candidate prostrates, he is blessed by the prior who blesses him with holy water. The name of the newly professed monk or converse is called during the Eucharistic Prayer. The ordination as a priest may follow two years later. A bishop and the entire family of the monk are invited.

Conclusion

Nobody can deny that Carthusian monks are sincere seekers of God, men who search for happiness and peace – like we all do. They are willing to make certain choices in their lives. St Bruno and his spiritual sons and daughters were driven by an inner fire. This fire led them to the desert. The world, with all kinds of distractions, only brought them agitation and confusion. The purity and nakedness of the desert – hard and merciless though it may seem – brought them God and therefore serenity and contentment.

Even today, Carthusian monks and nuns leave the world to realise this ancient ideal: they leave family and friends as well as ambition and wealth. The lifelong solitude and the great silence must 'empty' their spirits: empty from the sorrows of the world, in order to be 'filled' or 'fulfilled' by the love of God. Solitude was for Bruno and his disciples the most authentic way to a spiritual union with God, to become one with God. To achieve this ideal, Bruno designed a perfect balance between solitude and community. Therefore, the Carthusian order became a genuine reform of the monastic tradition. The community had to protect the hermit against despair or presumptuous holiness, in other words against acedia. Even today it takes time to adapt, sometimes a lifetime. 'Hard in the beginning, sweet at the end,' said Guigo I about stability in the cell. But the deeper significance of this ideal is only understood by those who are called to this kind of life.

Carthusian monks do not accomplish anything, they are of no direct use to the world, or even to the Church because they do not preach, or administer the sacraments to the faithful, or practise concrete charity. This is quite incomprehensible for most people, even for most Catholics. In the opinion of our competitive society it is completely incomprehensible, even idiotic! Like the biblical Mary, the sister of Martha, Carthusian monks and nuns sit at the feet of the Lord: they watch and listen, that is all they do. However, Mary had chosen the better part, had she not? How may these words of Jesus be understood? Free from utilitarianism, the Carthusian order – and all other monastic families, the Cistercians, the Trappists, the Camaldolese and the Carmelite orders – are to be understood as a kind of firehouse on the edge. The presence of God is often hard to find in postmodern society. Contemplatives are the silent and vigilant witnesses of deep truth, happiness and peace. Their hidden lives may be a call to recognise the sacred and invisible love of God in the world. As Cardinal Danneels said, Carthusian monks are the 'eyes of the hurricane': spots of total silence among the many storms which rage throughout the world and which destroy real happiness, calm and peace. 'Their humility, simplicity and silent presence are as a mirror for humanity. The consequent and persistent lifestyle is as a conscience for humanity and the Catholic Church. They confront us with the "ultimate truth" of a pure faith.'[203]

St Bruno may be the founder and father of the Carthusian order, but we ought not to underestimate the crucial role of Guigo I in the concrete formation and historic development of the entire order. A contemplative or spiritual life is impossible without rule, law and stability. Ingeniously, Guigo I conferred an enduring framework on the primitive observance of Bruno and his disciples by writing down *The Customs of Chartreuse*. He refined the original symbiosis between anchoretic and coenobitic monasticism with juridical underpinning. *The Customs of Chartreuse* concentrate all activities on the optimal experience of solitude and silence. The entire Carthusian life is directed to the contemplation of God: each prayer, each labour, every minute of the day, each movement. We hope that this book was able to give you a small taste of this reality.

---

[203] M. De Roeck, *Kardinaal Danneels over Into Great Silence*, p. 2.

Bibliography

X. Accart, 'Dans l'intimité d'une Chartreuse', *Prier* (2012/339), pp. 8–12.

G. Aerden, T. Peeters, 'Juiste omgang met de traditie behoedt het charisma voor verwatering. Het typevoorbeeld van het Gewoonteboek van Guigo de Kartuizer', *De Kovel. Monastiek Tijdschrift voor Vlaanderen en Nederland* (2012/21), pp. 18–30.

Algemeen Rijksarchief en Rijksarchief in de Provinciën, *Statuta ordinis cartusiensis a domino Guigone priore cartusie edita*, Bruxelles, 1998.

Fr André Prieur de Chartreuse, *Statuts de l'Ordre Cartusien. Approuvés par le Chapitre Général de 1987*, St-Pierre-de-Chartreuse, 1987.

B. Barrier, *Les activités du solitaire en chartreuse d'après les plus anciens témoins* (AC 87/1981).

P. Baud, *Des étincelles sur la neige. Textes des premiers frères chartreux*, Paris, 1999.

O. Beck (ed.), *Kartause Marienau. Ein Ort der Stille und des Gebets*, Thorbecke, 1990.

H.-J. Becker, *Die Responsorien des Kartäuserbreviers*, Munchen, 1971.

B. Bligny, *Recueil des plus anciens actes de la Grande Chartreuse*, Grenoble, 1958.

R. Bourgeois, *L'expulsion des Chartreux 29 avril 1903*, Grenoble, 2000.

S. Bruno – Guiges – S. Anthelme, *Lettres des premiers chartreux* (SC 88/1988).

T. Ceravolo, *Vita di San Bruno di Colonia. La ricerca di Dio nel silenzio del deserto*, Serra San Bruno, 2001.

Charterhouse of the Transfiguration, *Carthusian Nuns. In the name of all we remain in the presence of the living God*, Arlington (Vermont), 2006.

Charterhouse of the Transfiguration, *Carthusian Saints*, Arlington (Vermont), 2006.

Charterhouse of the Transfiguration, *Contemplatives in the Heart of the Church. The solemn teaching of Pope Pius XI on the apostolic value of Carthusian life*, Arlington (Vermont), 2006.

Congregation pour les Instituts de Vie Consacree et les Societes de Vie Apostolique, *La vie contemplative et la clôture des moniales. Instruction Verbi Sponsa 13 mai 1999*, Paris, 1999.

Correrie de la Grande Chartreuse, *L'ordre des chartreux*, St-Pierre-de-Chartreuse, 2002.

Correrie de la Grande Chartreuse, *Paroles de chartreux*, St-Pierre-de-Chartreuse, 2004.

G. M. Croce, M. Mulitzer, *Eremo Camaldolese di Monte Rua. Die Kamaldulenser Einsiedelei von Monte Rua* (AC 2011/274).

G. D'Alancon, *Saint Bruno. La solitude transfigurée*, Paris, 2011.

G. D'Alancon, *Saint Anthelme. Un chartreux devenu évêque*, Perpignan, 2013.

G. D'Angelo (ed.), *Certosini a Serra San Bruno. Nel silenzio la communione*, Milano, 2009.

G. Danneels, 'De laatste en de voorlaatste dingen', *in Abdij van Westmalle, Stilte aan het woord. Wandelen waar monniken wonen*, Westmalle, 1984, pp. 83–4.

G. Danneels, 'Het oog van de orkaan', in Abdij van Westmalle, *Stilte aan het woord. Wandelen waar monniken wonen*, Westmalle, 1984, pp. 11–21.

J. De Bruijn, 'De Gulden Brief nog leesbaar?', *Benedictijns Tijdschrift* (2001/3), pp. 115–35.

A. De Meyer, J. M. De Smet, 'Guigo's consuetudines van de eerste kartuizers', in *Mededelingen van de Koninklijke Vlaamse Academie voor wetenschap, letteren en schone kunsten van België XIII-6*, Brussels, 1951.

Denys le Chartreux, *Commentaire de l'Echelle du Paradis*, in *Opera Omnia. De oratione*, Tournai, 1902–13.

Denys le Chartreux, *Chroniques de l'extase. Textes choisis et présentés par Christophe Bagonneau* (Parole et Silence), 2000.

Denys le Chartreux, *Livre de vie des recluses* (Spir. Cart.), 2003.

Denys le Chartreux, *Vers la ressemblance. Textes choisis et présentés par Christophe Bagonneau* (Parole et Silence), 2003.

Denys le ChartreuX, *La vie et la fin du solitaire. Eloge de la vie en solitude* (Spir. Cart.), 2004.

M. De Roeck, *Kardinaal Danneels over Into Great Silence* (www.cinemien. nl), 2006, pp. 1–3.

E. De Smet, 'Zwijgend bestaan. Unieke maar bevreemde film over strenge kartuizerorde', *Kerk en Leven* (17 May 2006), p. 8.

A. Devaux, *Les origines du missel des chartreux* (AC 99/1995).

P. Drijvers, 'De weg naar het wezenlijke. Gesprek met de prior van La Grande Chartreuse, Marcellin Theeuwes o.c., door Samuel Pruvot, hoofdredacteur France Catholique', *Monastieke Informatie* (2004/211), pp. 102–18.

L. Fijen, *De reis van je hoofd naar je hart. Leefregels voor het bestaan van alledag*, Kampen, 2004.

T. Gaens, F. Timmermans (eds), *Liber Amicorum Jan Degrauwe* (AC 222/2004).

T. Gaens, J. De Grauwe, *De kracht van de stilte. Geest & Geschiedenis van de kartuizerorde*, Leuven, 2006.

T. Geyer, 'Is de Kartuizerregel niets anders dan de Regel van Sint-Benedictus, waaraan de Consuetudines van Dom Guigo en de daaropvolgende Statuten slechts eenvoudige Constituties zouden hebben toegevoegd?' Unpublished.

E. Ghini, *Oltre ogni limite. Nazarena monaca reclusa 1945–1990*, Roma, 2007.

G. Gioia, 'L'esperienza contemplativa. Bruno il certosino', in *Testi di San Bruno*, www.certosini.info.

G. Greshake, 'Bruno der Kartäuser', in *Lexicon fürThéologie und Kirche* (2/1996), col. 731–2.

Guiges I le Chartreux, *Coutumes de Chartreuse* (SC 313/1984).

Guiges I le Chartreux, *Vie de Saint Hugues. Evêque de Grenoble. L'ami des moines* (AC 112/1986).

Guiges I le Chartreux, *Méditations* (SC 308/2001).

Guiges II le Chartreux, *Lettre sur la vie contemplative (l'échelle des moines). Douze Méditations* (SC 163/2001).

Guigo De Kartuizer, *Gewoonten. Een leefregel voor kluizenaars in gemeenschap. Vertaling Tim Peeters en Guerric Aerden osco. Inleiding en annotatie Tim Peeters* (Serie Middeleeuwse Monastieke Teksten 4), Budel, 2011.

A. Guillerand, *Voix Cartusienne* (Parole et Silence), Paris, 2001.

A. Guillerand, *Vivantes clartés. Méditations cartusiennes* (Parole et Silence), Paris, 2002.

B. Hartmann, *De martelaren van Roermond*, Oegstgeest, 2009.

F. Hendrickx, T. Gaens, *Amo te, sacer ordo Carthusiensis. Jan De Grauwe, passioné de l'Ordre des Chartreux* (Miscellanea Neerlandica XXXVIII – Studia Cartusiana I), Leuven, 2012.

G. Hocquard, *Lettre du prieur Guiges Ier à un ami sur la vie solitaire* (AC 81/1980).

J. Hogg, A. Girard, D. le Blevec (eds), Statuta Ordinis Cartusiensis 1991 (AC 99/1992).

J. Hogg, A. Girard, D. le Blevec (eds), *The Evolution of the Carthusian Statutes from the 'Consuetudines Guigonis' to the 'tertia compilatio'* (AC 99/1992).

J. Hogg , A. Girard, D. Le Blevec (eds), *Der heilige Bruno von James Hogg* (AC 214/2003).

J. Hogg, A. Girard, D. le Blevec (eds), *Saint Bruno et sa postérité spirituelle* (AC 189/2003).

J. Hogg, A. Girard, D. Le Blevec (eds), *Saint Bruno en Chartreuse* (AC 192/2004).

J. Hogg, A. Girard, D. Le Blevec (eds), *Liber Amicorum James Hogg. Kartäuserforschung 1970–2006* (AC 210/2008).

J. Hollenstein, T. Lauko, *Wo die Stille spricht*, Kartause Pleterje, 1996.

A. Hoste, *De Regels voor reclusen en kluizenaars*, Steenbrugge, 2012.

I Monaci di Serra San Bruno, *Sentieri del deserto*, Soveria Mannelli, 2001.

John Paul II, *Vita Consecrata*, Vatican, 1994.

John Paul II, *Message du Saint Père à l'occasion du 9° Centenaire de la Mort de Saint Bruno*, Vatican, 14 May 2001.

J.-C. Krikorian (ed.), *La tradition vivante. Saint Bruno et les chartreux. Roulent les mondes, la Croix demeure. Stat Crux dum volvitur orbis*, Paris, 1999.

La Certosa Serra San Bruno (ed.), *I colori del silenzio. The colors of silence. La Certosa di Serra San Bruno. The Charterhouse of Serra San Bruno*, Serra San Bruno, 2000.

La Certosa Serra San Bruno (ed.), *San Bruno e i certosini*, Serra San Bruno, 2001.

J.-J. Lansperge, 'Epistolae paraeneticae ac morales', in *Opera Omnia*, Montreuil-sur-Mer, 1880–90.

M. Laporte, 'Aux sources de la vie cartusienne. Traits fondamentaux de la Chartreuse' (unpublished source from the Great Charterhouse), 1960–65.

L. A. Lassus, *Saint Romuald. L'ermite-Prophète*, Le Barroux, 1991.

L. A. Lassus, *Nazarena. Une recluse au cœur de Rome 1907–1990*, Le Barroux, 1996.

B. Lauvrijs, *Onbekende, kerkelijk erkende roepingen. Gewijde kluizenaars, maagden/weduwen, sociëteiten van apostolisch leven en nieuwe bewegingen: vergelijking met de religieuzen*, Westerlo, 2001.

D. Le Blevec, 'Un érémitisme tempéré', in *La voie cartusienne. Une vie cachée en Dieu* (Carmel, 107/2003), pp. 11–19.

J. Leflon, *Un haut lieu d'Ardenne. Le Mont Saint-Walfroy*, Charleville-Mézières, 1960.

Les Chartreux, *Chemins vers le silence intérieur. La contemplation* (Parole et Silence), 1987.

Les Moines de Portes, *Lettres des premiers chartreux II* (SC 274/1999).

S. Lieven, 'Série d'été 8/8. Dans le silence des abbayes', *Pèlerin* (2011/6716), pp. 26–36.

A. Louf, *San Bruno l'esperienza del deserto*, Serra San Bruno, 2001.

A. Louf (tr. S. Yucom), 'Saint Bruno', *Cistercian Studies Quarterly* (48/2013), pp. 213–24, 353–67.

L. Madelon, *La Chartreuse de Portes* (Ain), Lyon, 1996.

T. Matus, *Nazarena. Una monaca reclusa nella comunità camaldolese*, Camaldoli, 1998.

T. Matus, *Alle origini di Camaldoli. San Romualdo e i cinque fratelli*, Camaldoli, 2003.

G. Mursell, *The Theology of the Carthusian Life in the Writings of St Bruno and Guigo I* (AC 127/1988).

Musée Dauphinois (ed.), *La Grande Chartreuse. Au-delà du silence*, Glénat, 2002.

N. Nabert, *Les Larmes, la Nourriture, le Silence* (Spir. Cart.), 2001.

N. Nabert, 'L'ascese du corps', *La Voie cartusienne. Une vie cachée en Dieu* (Carmel, 107/2003), pp. 21–41.

N. Nabert, 'Louange et vie contemplative', *La Voie cartusienne. Une vie cachée en Dieu* (Carmel, 107/2003), pp. 73–97.

N. Nabert, 'Prologue: un ministère d'union divine', *La Voie cartusienne. Une vie cachée en Dieu* (Carmel, 107/2003), pp. 5–8.

N. Nabert (sous la direction), *Tristesse, acédie et médicine des âmes. Anthologie de textes rares et inédits (XIIIe–XXe siècle)* (Spir. Cart.), 2005.

N. Nabert, *Le commentaire des psaumes des montées, une échelle de vie intérieure* (Spir. Cart.), 2006.

N. Nabert, *Rites et paroles de la profession solennelle dans l'Ordre des Chartreux* (AC 253/2007), pp. 11–21.

N. Nabert, *Des jardins d'herbes et d'âme* (Spir. Cart.), 2007.

N. Nabert, *La Figure de Marie en Chartreuse. Une dormition de la Vierge, manuscrit inédit de la Grande-Chartreuse* (Spir. Cart.), 2008.

N. Nabert, *Les moniales chartreuses*, Genève, 2009.

W. Nigg, *Het geheim der monniken*, Amsterdam, 1954.

P. Nissen, 'Bruno van Keulen: geroepen tot vriendschap en eenzaamheid', *Benedictijns Tijdschrift* (1984/3), pp.78–97.

P. Nissen, 'Eenzaamheid als zoeken van God', *Benedictijns Tijdschrift* (2001/3), pp. 91-103.

Octavo (ed.), *Camaldoli. Sacro Eremo e Monastero*, Firenze, 2000.

K. Pansters (ed.), *Het geheim van de stilte. De besloten wereld van de Roermondse Kartuizers*, Roermond, 2009.

T. Peeters, 'O beata solitudo, o sola beatitudo. Het solitaire leven van Sint Bruno en de kartuizers', *Collationes* 33 (2003), pp. 73–91.

T. Peeters, *Gods eenzame zwijgers. De spirituele weg van de kartuizers*, Gent, Carmelitana, 2007.

T. Peeters, 'Leven in het hart van de Kerk: de kartuizers en de kerkelijke communio', *Communio* (2007/5–6), pp. 422–31.

T. Peeters, *Vivere nel cuore della Chiesa: i certosini e la 'communio' ecclesiale* (AC 267/2008), pp. 29–42.

T. Peeters, 'De ene spiritualiteit van Jezus en de vele spirituele wegen tot navolging. Mijmeringen na een bezoek aan de prior van La Grande Chartreuse', *Emmaüs, voor wie met Christus door de tijd wil gaan* (April–May 2009), pp. 5–13.

T. Peeters, 'De kartuizerorde en het benedictijns monnikendom: twijgen aan dezelfde stronk?', *De Kovel. Monastiek Tijdschrift voor Vlaanderen en Nederland* (2009/6), pp. 8–14.

T. Peeters, 'Vivere nel cuore della Chiesa: i certosini e la 'communio' ecclesiale', *Claretianum. Commentaria Theologica Opera et Studio Instituti Theologiae Vitae Consecratae*, Roma (XLIX/2009), pp. 195–206.

T. Peeters, 'De heilige Bruno achterna: getuigenis van een bijzondere roeping', *Het Teken* (November 2010), pp. 139–42.

T. Peeters, 'L'Ordre des Chartreux et le monachisme bénédictin: une branche au même tronc?', *Collectanea Cisterciensia. Revue de Spiritualité Monastique*, (72/2010/3), pp. 319–26.

T. Peeters, *La voie spirituelle des Chartreux*, Paris, 2010.

T. Peeters, 'Monastieke Familie van Bethlehem wordt zestig. Gastvrije gemeenschap van solitairen', *Tertio* 559 (27 October 2010), p. 10.

T. Peeters, *Quando il silenzio parla. La vita dei certosini*, Milano, 2011.

T. Peeters, 'Camaldulenzen vieren milleniumfeest. Duizend jaar als één dag', *De Kovel. Monastiek Tijdschrift voor Vlaanderen en Nederland* (2012/23), pp. 62–72.

T. Peeters, 'Milles ans sont comme un jour. Les camaldules fêtent leur millénaire', *Collectanea Cisterciensia. Revue de Spiritualité Monastique* (74/2012/3), pp. 305–12.

T. Peeters, 'Dossier: Duizend jaar Camaldoli', *Tertio* 644 (13 June 2012), pp. 8–9.

T. Peeters, 'Kartuizerinnen op zoek naar stabiele observantie: relaas van een lang geboorteverhaal', *De Kovel. Monastiek Tijdschrift voor Vlaanderen en Nederland* (2014/34), pp. 50–61.

J. Picard, *La Grande Chartreuse et les chartreuses de Portes, Sélignac et Pierre Chatel* (AC 61/1986).

Pius XI, *Umbratilem. Constitutions Apostolique de notre Très Saint Père le pape Pie XI approuvant les Statuts de l'Ordre des Chartreux*, 1924.

S. Pruvot, '900e anniversaire de la mort de saint Bruno. L'univers cartusien', *France Catholique* (2001/2796), pp. 12–18.

S. Pruvot, 'Entretien avec Dom Marcellin', *France Catholique* (2004/2915), pp. 8–15.

A. Ravier, *L'approche de Dieu. Par le silence de solitude*, Saint Laurent du Pont, 1996.

A. Ravier, *Le premier ermitage des moines de Chartreuse. Juin 1084-30 janvier 1132*, Saint-Pierre-de-Chartreuse, 2001.

A. Ravier, *Saint Bruno le Chartreux*, Paris, 2003.

J. Reijnders, *Een reis in stilte. Leven als kartuizers*, Kampen, 2006.

E. Romeo, *I solitari di Dio. Separati da tutto, uniti a tutti*, Catanzaro, 2005.

H. J. Roth, 'Sind die Kartäuser Benediktiener?', *Erbe und Auftrag* (50/1974) pp. 55–7.

Saint Pierre Damien, Saint Bruno de Querfurt, *La vie du bienheureux Romuald. La vie des cinq frères. Textes traduit par le Père L.A. Lassus. Introduction par le Rme Père D. Giabbani*, Namur, 1962.

T. H. M. Schaik, *Het kroost van broeder Joost. Waarom de kartuizers niet terugkwamen naar Nederland*, Kampen, 2007.

Secretariat general de la conference des eveques de France (ed.), 'Saint Bruno', in *Documents Episcopat* (12–13/2001), pp. 1–18.

R. Serrou, P. Vals, *Au 'désert' de Chartreuse. La vie solitaire des fils de saint Bruno*, Evreux, 1996.

Sint Willibrordusabdij (ed.), *Sint Benedictus' Regel voor monniken*, Slangenburg, 1989.

M. Theeuwes, 'Bruno van Keulen. Ervaring en traditie', *Benedictijns Tijdschrift* (2001/3), pp. 104–11.

F. Timmermans, T. Gaens (eds), *Magister Bruno. Negen eeuwen uitstraling van de kartuizerorde*, Leuven, 2003.

K. Thir, *Einsamkeit und schweigen als wege zu Gottwirken und Botschaft der Kartäuser* (AC 83/1995).

Un Certosino, *Ferventi d'amore divino. Meditazioni su San Bruno*, Serra San Bruno, 2002.

Un Chartreux, 'Solitude et sainteté', *La Vie spirituelle*, Paris, 1960.

Un Chartreux, *Maître Bruno, père des Chartreux* (AC 115/1990).

Un Chartreux, *La Grande Chartreuse par un Chartreux*, Bellegarde, 1998.

Un Chartreux, *Écoles de silence* (Parole et Silence), Paris, 2001.

Un Chartreux, *Vivre dans l'intimité du Christ*, Paris, tome 1 (2005); tome 2 (2006).

Un Chartreux, 'Silence et solitude: une vie de Chartreux', *Études. Revue de culture contemporaine* (July–August 2007), pp. 63–74.

Un Chartreux, *L'echo du silence*, Perpignan, 2012.

Une Moniale de la Chartreuse Notre-Dame, *Prier 15 jours avec saint Bruno, fondateur des chartreux*, Montrouge, 2001.

W. Van Der Horst, *Daniël de pilaarheilige (409–493). Zijn levensbeschrijving uit het Grieks vertaald en toegelicht*, Averbode, 2009.

P. Van Der Meer de Walcheren, *Het witte paradijs*, Utrecht, 1948.

P. Van de Vyvere, 'Opgrimbie … anders. Het leven van de monialen van Bethlehem', *Kerk en Leven* (17 February 1999), p. 20.

J. Vranckx, 'Ik was een kartuizer', *Gazet van Antwerpen* (2–3 September 2006), pp. 4–5.